HOW TO SUCCESSF

EVALUATE AND MARKET YOUR

MARKETING BASICS

FOR YOUR SMALL BUSINESS

JEN ESPARZA

Marketing Basics for Your Small Business
Copyright © 2022 Jen Esparza

All rights reserved. No part of this publication may be reproduced, distributed or transmitted in any form or by any means, including photocopying, recording, or other electronic or mechanical methods, without the prior written permission of the publisher, except in the case of brief quotations embodied in reviews and certain other noncommercial uses permitted by copyright law.

Adherence to all applicable laws and regulations, including international, federal, state and local governing professional licensing, business practices, advertising, and all other aspects of doing business in the US, Canada or any other jurisdiction is the sole responsibility of the reader and consumer.

Requests for information should be sent to, jen@thejenadvantage.com

Library of Congress Control Number: 2022917365

ISBN: 979-8-9867310-0-1

For Joe, Elena and Joey

Thank you for supporting my dream, being my inspiration and never giving up on me.

Get your **FREE** worksheets to accompany the exercises in this book!

You may find that the room to write in the book isn't enough, or maybe you don't want to mess up the pretty pages. Within the worksheets you'll find plenty of space to brainstorm, doodle and dream of marketing ideas for your business.

Download your free worksheets at:

thejenadvantage.com

Contents

Introduction 1

Part 1 5
Business Assessment

1. Business Evaluation 7
2. Assessing Your Competition 17
3. Who Are Your Customers? 21
4. Customer Retention 27
5. Marketing Budget 33
6. Your Company Image 37

Part 2 45
Marketing

Free marketing 51

7. Online Reviews and Referrals 53
8. Google Business Profile 59
9. Free Options in Traditional Media 61
10. All Things Social Media 67

Paid marketing 95

11. Your Business Website 97

12. Digital Marketing 105
13. Paid Advertising and Event Opportunities 115
14. Printed Marketing Material 121
15. Hiring a Professional 125
Part 3 129
Your Marketing Strategy
16. Implementing Marketing Strategies 131

Introduction

If you're a small business owner trying to understand how to market your business, you're in the right place.

You're not going to find jargon, buzzwords or gimmicks in this book—marketing does not need to feel like a mystery. You are going to find manageable tasks that will help you build a stronger business and give the right message to the right people. I know that "small business" is a broad term. A hairstylist, a car mechanic and a florist pick up this book . . . yes, it sounds like the beginning of a bad joke. But while I'm aware that your businesses may be vastly different, the marketing tools you need to define your demographic, refine your mission and reach customers are the same.

Please do not discredit yourself by thinking, "But I'm just a [baker, mechanic, fill in the blank]." If you're trying to make money, you need marketing. If business is booming, you may think that marketing can wait. But the marketing you do now prepares you for when business is slow so that you've got an email list to contact, a social media following to reach out to and a loyal customer base to depend on.

I have provided marketing to a spectrum of businesses from government programs to children's theater, but marketing for small businesses makes my heart sing.

Every small business owner I meet has a dozen balls in the air and a dream and the drive to keep at it every day. I admire you. You are hardworking. You are dedicated. You are rare. And any way that I can support your business, I'm here for it. I wrote this for you.

When I began research for writing this book, I was unimpressed with the competition. I found books upward of 400–500 pages long on marketing that gave detail and data that no small business owner would ever need. You don't have time for 500 pages. What you need are clear steps that help you create a solid foundation and offer marketing solutions that make sense. If you're willing to work on your authentic self and sell a reliable product/service, you'll have no problem implementing these marketing strategies.

This book won't be for everyone, and that's OK. I'm going to ask you to look at the heart of your business and adjust to make room for new things. If you were looking for an answer to get rich quickly, you won't find it here. If you're looking to build your client base, earn more and build a solid business by implementing the right marketing strategies, then let's dive in.

The need for marketing

You may be the best plumber, run the cutest coffee shop or be the most talented barber in the business, but none of that matters if nobody knows about you. You can do business with your neighbors and your family and get a few referrals from them, but then what? How do people find and choose you?

A simple internet search shows more than 50 plumbers in my general area. As a consumer I think, "How do I choose?" As an owner, you may worry how they will ever choose you.

This is why you're going to market your business. Effective marketing is arguably the most critical component of any thriving business. It's what attracts potential customers to your brand and creates name recognition, and it's how you'll be remembered over time. (Sneak peek: marketing doesn't stop when the appointment book is full!) If you're thinking you have no idea what you're doing, I'm honestly relieved because, otherwise, you wouldn't need me.

I'm not here to waste your time. You already know that a huge percentage of the population uses social media, you know that magazines offer advertising and, even in this music-streaming era, you know that radio commercials still exist. I don't think you need a book to tell you what marketing is. I offer you something different. I want to show you how to do it—in bite-size chunks that are achievable and have an impact. But before we can even talk about the *how*, we need to talk about the *why*.

This marketing book is different in that it begins with an evaluation. You must know what you're selling, why you're in business and who your target audience is before you can market anything.

This unique concept will ensure your business is built on a solid foundation before you begin marketing. I can promise you that if you care about your why as much as your profit, you're going to be more successful.

I can promise you that if you care about your why as much as your profit, you're going to be more successful.

A quick note about independent contractors

If you are an independent contractor, you may think that these marketing strategies won't work for you since you don't own your own business. But many of the strategies are similar, so you will find that this book *is* for you. My nephew is a barber, which presents a weird situation. He rents his space and brings in his own clients, but sometimes he takes the walk-in customers without appointments. He doesn't own the business, but he needs to build a name for himself. So for him, a Google Business Profile doesn't apply. He could create a Yelp page, but he really doesn't have his own business. In his case, he uses Instagram to promote himself. He posts photos of haircuts that he does, reminding people of his hours and letting followers know when he's got an opening. Similarly, insurance agents or car salesmen work largely on commission but work under the umbrella of an agency name. You may not be a small business owner, but your business depends on how you market yourself, so many of these strategies will still apply. If you aren't the one who can make decisions about advertising or event sponsorship, brainstorm what makes sense for your business and pitch the idea to the people who *do* make the decision.

Part 1

Business Assessment

Well, hello, fellow small business owner. I know as well as you that being a small business owner is a big accomplishment. I applaud you for your tenacity! On one hand, being your own boss can be exciting. Nobody is telling you when to arrive at work or denying a request for time off. But there is so much to do, who has time for a day off? On top of your own work, being a business owner also comes with responsibilities that most don't enjoy like accounting, human resources and the reason you're reading—marketing.

I complete an evaluation with each new client, and I believe it's the most important tool to set yourself up for successful marketing. Since marketing, broadly defined as "promoting and selling products," can be costly and ineffective if not done correctly, it's important to first evaluate your business to determine what you need. Consider this the beginning piece of the marketing plan we're creating. You'll get an overview of your business, your audience, your competition, your budget and your goals. Then we'll explore dozens of marketing strategies and finish up with deciding which ones are best for you.

The next few pages will likely take you a few hours to complete, but you don't have to do it all at once. These questions are simple but designed to make you think deeply. You may want to get a piece of paper or open a new document on your computer to write out your answers. The best tools you can use for this are the free worksheets available to download on thejenadvantag e.com.

The business you have built is too valuable to skip the writing exercises in this book. I cannot stress enough how important it is that you make this effort for the good of your business. You owe it to yourself to create the time and space to be thoughtful about your marketing strategies.

1

Business Evaluation

What is your business?

I asked a client this, and he said, "Well, I'm an electrician." If you're not an electrician, you might not know what an open-ended statement this is. I knew he was an electrician, but I wanted to know *what* he did. "Oh," he said, "we specialize in installing electric vehicle chargers, solar panels and whole-house batteries." Now *that*'s what I was truly asking. Because whatever your industry, chances are you have some specialties. Before he focused on those services, his niche was actually creating smart homes for a targeted audience of older adults who needed help with installing smart thermostats, programming remotes or installing home security. Now his clients are more affluent, eco-conscious individuals, ranging in age and ethnicity. To just say "I'm an electrician" doesn't narrow down your niche and your audience. To say "I'm a baker" doesn't narrow it down to fine pastries or bread. To say "I roast coffee" doesn't say if you sell it wholesale in bulk, package it for individual customers or sell it freshly brewed at a coffee shop.

I think you get the idea to really consider what it is that you do.

What is your business?

What is your value proposition?

This is just a fancy way of asking what makes your business special. Your value proposition convinces potential customers why your product or service will add value or solve a problem better than any other similar offering. This may be a simple statement, it may be a bullet point list or it may be your company's tagline. The bottom line is if you can't come up with reasons why you're valuable, how will your customers? If you don't have a value proposition already composed, brainstorm ideas and phrases to begin crafting your statement.

When I brainstormed mine, I came up with words like personal, integrity and authenticity. My value proposition: The Jen Advantage is individual attention given to your business that provides you personalized solutions to achieve your marketing goals.

My business cards have a snapshot of that: authentic communication and marketing solutions for small businesses and nonprofits.

What is your value proposition?

What is your why?

I'll go first. I am in marketing because I know how to produce compelling marketing materials. The end.

Just kidding. That might be part of the answer, but remember, we're taking a deeper dive here. Personally, I got into helping small businesses because I saw a need. I saw small business owners who had integrity and passion and great skill yet were stretched so thin that they couldn't possibly come up with the energy to write a catchy social post or make sense of Google Ads at the end of the day. When I was fresh out of college and in the professional world, my first boss told me that my job was to "keep the monkeys off his back," meaning that it was my job to play defense for him. I had the authority to answer questions and make decisions about issues (the monkeys) and was only to come to him when all of my resources were exhausted. That's how I still feel. It's my job to know all things marketing for my clients to keep that monkey off their back. Providing that relief to let these good people just "do their job" feels amazing. Ah, yes, *that* is why I got into this business.

We all have bills to pay—that's one reason why we get out of bed each morning. But you don't just go to work; you run a business. What made you start this business? Why do you love it enough that you're reading a book and doing an exercise to make it better?

What is your why?

What would you like to do more of?

So far you've established what you do and why you do it. Were you surprised at either of your answers? As a small business owner, it is so easy to get wrapped up in the day-to-day grind of appointments, new clients, taking calls, sending bills, balancing invoices and on and on that you can lose focus on these things.

Now that you've revisited what you do and why you do it, what would you like to do more of? I love the answers that come from this question. This could go in multiple directions. I had one client tell me, "I want to fish more." He wanted to hire enough help and have his business be financially fluid enough that he could take off days to fish. Then a landscape designer told me she wished she could do more creative work—like really unique designs beyond your basic grass and flowers. A café may wish to expand hours to serve beyond their current lunch service; a carpet cleaner may wish they could branch out into other cleaning services to expand their offerings. I'll tell you mine. I wish I could help more small businesses. But I am only one person who only has so many hours in a day, which limits how many clients I can actually work with. So that is how the idea for this book was born, and here we are.

Whether it be personal or professional, what would you like to do more of?

What makes you the most money?

We can talk about what makes us warm and fuzzy and makes us love our job all day long, but at the end of the day, bills need to be paid. Of all the things your business offers, what are your biggest income producers? Is it repeat clients or maybe product add-ons sold on-site? If you own a restaurant, is it a particular food? If you're a hairstylist, a certain service? I encourage you to look at the complete picture of cost and profit.

A restaurant owner I spoke with said that he made a great return on his homemade chicken pot pies. They were inexpensive to make, but people paid top dollar. The downside was that if they didn't get cooked and eaten in a short period of time, they would become unusable. Instead of great profit, he'd break even or possibly have a loss. So this was a risk/reward situation. After testing various menu combinations, he was able to justify the "risk" by offering other menu items that had a longer shelf life and had very little risk. Financially, he still came out on top, and when those pies sold, his profits were incredible. Your business may be more straightforward and present situations with no risk.

I once had a carpet cleaning scheduled, and the estimate was somewhere around $250. The technician offered to add a protectant and stain remover to each room, which would raise the cost to $450. What an easy way to double the sale! We could get into sales ethics here, which I won't except to say there is a time and a place for upselling. I wasn't a fan of this situation because it was completely unnecessary for my home. However, there are plenty of times the strategy has its place and helps the customer. The place you make the most money may be from the add-on options that you offer.

Remember to keep in mind the cost of materials and time involved to determine your profit.

What makes you the most money?

Does your biggest moneymaker coincide with what you like to do?

You now have a full picture of what you do, what you'd like to do more of and what makes you the most money. But you should also consider: Do you like the thing that makes you the most money? Is it going well, and do you want to keep focusing on it? Or do you wish something else was your main income source? Perhaps you'd prefer to take your company in a different direction. You've got a really great base here to think critically about your business and begin to focus on the direction you want to take it from here. Initially with my business, what made me the most money did not correlate with what I love to do. So I had to really examine my business model after that realization. You know what I love to do? Write. Using my own advice to take inventory of my business once in a while has proved quite helpful!

Does your biggest moneymaker coincide with what you like to do? If not, how can you reconfigure your business to change this?

Where does your business come from?

If you don't track where your business comes from, you absolutely should. I mentioned it before, and I will say it multiple times: marketing can be a waste of money if you don't do it right. I have seen small businesses throw thousands of dollars at gimmick marketing and then never know if it even produced leads. I am so glad that you're here because you're going to learn from their mistakes.

If you don't track where your leads come from, start now. If you use any kind of scheduling software, a feature is likely built into it where you can ask customers how they heard of you. If you're using a paper calendar to make your appointments, then you'll need a simple spreadsheet with columns and checkboxes to help you track the information. Your data collection does not need to be fancy; you just need to do it. Where might your customers hear from you? Facebook, friend referral, mailbox flyer, internet search? Whatever the options, add those to your spreadsheet columns and start making tally marks. This information is going to tell you what is working well and what needs some help. Is your business based on walk-in clients? That's OK; you can still ask and keep the same tally sheet to check off. Do you have analytics for your website and social media? Gather all of it. Look at your data and take the time to analyze it. Knowing where the business comes from helps you determine if you need to spend more time on internet advertising, community outreach events, referral programs, etc.

Where does your business come from?

What kind of philanthropy are you doing?

It never ceases to amaze me that busy business owners still find time to give back to their community. When I ask new clients if they are involved in philanthropy, more often than not they list half a dozen (or more!) community organizations and charities they are involved with. I promise there is no shame in keeping your gifting to one or two organizations, but I have found that this is a very important piece of the "successful small business" puzzle. Giving back to the community is a great way to share your generosity and project your company as a caring one.

I know a business owner who loves cats. They use a cat in their logo, and their newsletter is written from the cat's perspective. So it only made sense that they sponsor the adoption of a cat each month. For you, this may look like sponsoring a local 5K or a children's sports team or donating products to charity fundraisers. Instead of monetary contributions, you may consider donating your time to a nonprofit board or arranging a team volunteer day like a creek cleanup in the community with your staff. Not only does giving back feel good but also it's important to reach the communities you serve through ways other than ads that ask them to buy your product/use your service.

What kind of philanthropy are you doing (and if you're not doing any, where can you start)?

What are your goals?

You may have addressed your goals a bit in the "what would you like to do more of" section, but this is a little different.

You might want more customers or more free time, but what are some goals that will help you measure your progress? Determine your goals for the next six months, one year, three years and beyond. When I started working with a new client, he told me he wanted to sell his business and retire in three years. We set some very measurable goals so that when he sells his company, it will be worth the amount he's hoping to sell it for. Another client wants to grow by one technician/truck per year. There are more financial details within that goal, but it's a great place to start. From a goal like that, you can begin to figure out what your income needs to be to achieve it.

Your goals may be based on growth by customer base, new locations, more employees, implementing raises, etc. But remember to keep them measurable because that will be how you know you achieved them. Wanting to be the restaurant where everyone goes for romantic and celebratory dinners is a great idea, but how will you know you've achieved it? If you're busy every night but barely making payroll, that goal doesn't really matter. When you set measurable goals, you balance the overall goal (I want everyone to come to my restaurant) with the practical goal (I need to hit 80 percent capacity every night and make a 200 percent profit). When you reach those financial goals, chances are that will mean you've hit your overall goals. The best way to ensure your goals are measurable is to create "smart" goals. Specific, Measurable, Achievable, Relevent, Time-Bound (SMART). (Psst, if you haven't downloaded them yet, the free worksheets on thejenadvantage.com are a great resource for this exercise!)

When you answer this question, consider your goals for the next six months, one year, three years and beyond.

What are your goals?

This evaluation tool helps you get a solid grasp of your business before moving on. In the next step, we're going to talk about your image to make sure that this awesome business you've created is seen just as you hope it is.

KEY TAKEAWAY: I need to evaluate my business and set goals before creating a marketing plan so I know what I need to market.

This exercise will prove useful as you continue the activities throughout the rest of the book. You may need to refer to it, so keep it handy.

☐ I have completed my business evaluation. The most interesting thing I realized was:

Assessing Your Competition

There are dozens of restaurants, hundreds of house painters and thousands of books—what makes each one special?

You need to take the time to think about your competition. Who else in your area is doing what you do? In case you are in a niche business, before you say nobody, hold on. I know a family who owns the only coffee shop in a small town. So they had to look a little broader. There were a handful of restaurants in the same area. What if one of them decided to start serving breakfast? Were they prepared to compete? Eventually, they decided to try out staying open late on the weekends but were overwhelmed by the competition from nearby breweries. They added an open mic night, and suddenly, they had something to set them apart again.

This is one reason you evaluated your business. When it's time to grow, improve or pivot, a solid foundation is critical.

Back to the competition. Who is it? For the sake of this exercise, say you're a general contractor. You know there are others in your surrounding area, but whose names do you hear most? Do you have a mentor who taught you the trade? Do you have other friends in the industry that you refer work to or get work from? Is there someone plastering their name on every city bus and mailer? Is there someone in the area that you really respect and model your business after?

Somewhere in all of those questions, you will find your answer. Find two companies that are equal/direct competitors and one that is really extraordinary. The equal competitors are about the same size and do about the same thing as you. The extraordinary one may be larger, do more or have been around longer. This one is the dream competition—maybe the one you hope to be someday.

Note: bigger is *not* better. I asked a hairstylist this question, and her ultimate competition was a stylist in New York City. She never really intended to make it to *that* level, but she loved so many things about her. She loved the excellent reputation she had, she loved that she was revered and taken seriously in the industry and she loved the array of social media this woman posted. Just because her goal wasn't to become a stylist in New York didn't mean she couldn't still take all the elements that she admired and implement them in her own business.

Exercise:

For this exercise, you can write here or download the worksheet from thejenadvantage.com.

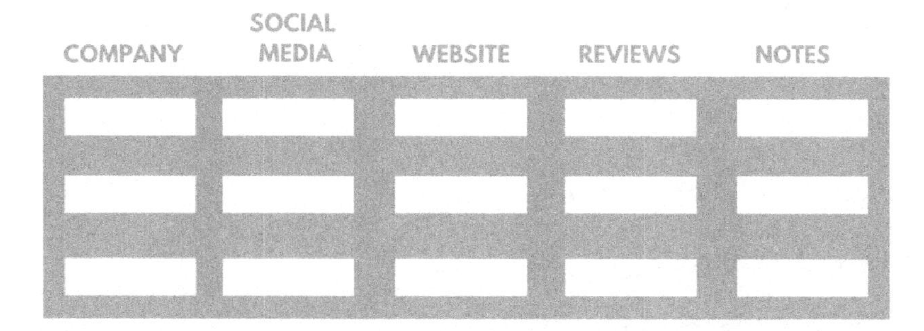

Fill in the chart for each competitor. This is a preview of the topics that we are going to cover in just a little bit. But before we dive in, I want you to briefly research each company and compare them to yourself.

How are you similar/different? What sets you apart? Make me hire you! Make me want to eat at your café! What sets you apart from your direct competition? Think cleanliness, quality, price, etc.

Now, analyze their marketing:

Social media

•Are they on social media?

•Which channels?

•Do they post frequently?

•Are the posts relevant?

•How does this compare to you?

Website

•Do they have a website?

•Is it easy to navigate?

•Is it clear what they do and how to contact them?

•How does this compare to you?

Online Reviews

Visit online review platforms like Google, Yelp and Nextdoor.

•Do they have reviews?

•Are they good?

•Do they respond?

•How does this compare to you?

In each box put a plus sign if they are doing something better than you, an equal sign if they are the same and a minus sign if they are performing below you. But feel free to take notes when you see something you like!

It's important to revisit this exercise annually so you can keep a pulse on what your competitors are doing. Keep an eye out to see if they've found a new technology to use that makes the job easier or if they offer a new service that you hadn't thought to implement, etc.

One last word about competition: it shouldn't feel like a bad thing. One doctor couldn't possibly see every patient in an entire city alone, right? It's OK that others do what you do. And, hopefully, they do it well. There is nothing like a bad contractor to give all contractors a bad rap. Competition encourages you to do your best, to continue learning and to hold yourself accountable to your processes to stay on top.

KEY TAKEAWAY: It's key to understand my competition so I can continue to improve in my industry.

☐ I understand who my competitors are. One thing I'd like to change to keep up with my competition is:

3

Who Are Your Customers?

When was the last time you stopped to consider who your customers are—your customer demographics? Along with tracking where your business comes from, you should track your customer demographics.

Why? Because you need to know who you're marketing to. Age, gender, earning status and place they live all impact how you market. As I write this, I feel like I am divulging some super-secret marketing trick. Knowing these demographics is important. It doesn't make you racist or discriminatory; instead, it helps you speak loudest to the people most likely to buy your product/service. Would you put a hearing aid commercial on during cartoon programming? No, that would be a waste of money.

It's not surprising that a fishing tackle store would advertise in Field & Stream instead of Good Housekeeping. They know their target audience is more likely to read one over the other. That doesn't mean that a woman who reads Good Housekeeping can't love fishing or be married to an avid fisherman. It just means that businesses, especially small ones, only have so many resources, so they have to choose where and how to spend them wisely.

When I ran the advertising for a children's theater company, we advertised in a local magazine because they reached a broad range of our demographic. The readers might have children to enroll in our theater, they may be teachers who want to bring their class on a field trip to see us or they may love theater and want to come see a show. We chose this magazine over one in a nearby retirement community. This retirement community had a great circulation, but their advertising only reached a piece of our demographic (those who might come see a show). With enough money for just one ad, the local magazine made more sense.

Just know that your demographic can change when politics, the economy or a pandemic turns the world on its head. In early 2008 an upscale restaurant opened up. They offered expensive menu items—somewhere you dressed up and went to for special occasions. Then the recession hit, and it sidelined them. Many of their previous customers no longer had the disposable income to eat and drink lavishly. Their options were to shut down or pivot. To stay in business, the restaurant completely changed its model. They changed to an "order at the counter" establishment and added more comfort food on the menu since the recession was a time in need of comfort, not overindulgence. It was a success. While it was never the business they intended on building, when their target market changed (from having disposable income to being on a tight budget), they had to change with them. Had they not catered (no pun intended) to the change in their customers, the restaurant would have failed.

Similarly, I know a great little antique store. Most of their shoppers are women who are over 50. Since these women are primarily retired and run their errands in the morning, the store is busiest then. They used to stay open until 8 p.m., but their evening hours didn't get enough customers to justify the cost, so they changed to closing at 5 p.m. Still wanting to serve their customers who worked day jobs, they expanded to being open on the weekends. This way they were able to have better staffing in the morning and still accommodate other customers on the weekend. Without doing an exercise on their demographic, they may have never found the right answer to their problem.

Their customer profile looks something like this:

Demographic

•50+

•suburban

•retired

Interests

•entertaining

•travel

•history

Needs

•variety

•products that are relevant

Barriers

•fixed income

•shops when fewer people are out

Motivations

•unique items

•value priced

•personal connection

Exercise:

Create a customer profile either on the downloadable worksheets or in the same document you created for your business assessment. Consider your average customer. Fill in the information in each category. If you service a couple of vastly different clients (residential and commercial, parents and child, etc.), feel free to create more than one.

Demographic: Age, race, gender, marital status, income, education, employment.

Interests: What are their interests, hobbies, things of importance to them?

Needs: What do they need from you or in general?

Barriers: What might keep them from getting what they need?

Motivation: What will motivate them to choose your business?

Questions to consider when exploring your demographic:

•What age do I serve? Are my customers under 30 or over 65?

•Are they families or singles?

•Are they homeowners?

•Do they have discretionary money, or are they on a strict budget?

•What are their personality traits?

This, of course, doesn't show a *full* picture of who you serve, but it helps create a focus when it comes time to target your marketing effort.

KEY TAKEAWAY: Knowing my customer demographic helps me target my marketing with the right message to the right people.

□ I completed my customer profile. I learned:

Customer Retention

Since customers are literally how you continue to exist, it's important that you prioritize customer retention. Depending on how you market, customer leads can cost a lot of money. Once you have the opportunity to serve a customer, you should be doing everything you can to retain them.

Current customers

A common mistake for small business owners is to focus all their efforts on building new business and forget the customers they already have. While you're trying to attract new leads, don't underestimate the power of a current customer. People become emotionally connected when they spend money with you. You hope this means they loved the experience and tell everyone how great you are. The last time I switched hairstylists I took a huge risk going to someone new and absolutely loved her. She was a great person, and I was happy with the results. I immediately posted her card on my social media, and I told at least a dozen people about her within a month of my visit. This is what we hope and pray all of our customers do. Most of your customers aren't in the marketing business and nutty like me, so you might have to work at it a bit. But you've got a captive audience, so don't ignore them!

You already got them to make the biggest leap and that was to dine at your restaurant, use your service, etc. How do you get them to come back for more? The restaurant may have a frequent diner discount card, the realtor might make follow-up calls to check on the new homeowners or the window washer might offer a discount on another service they offer to past customers. It could be a lot of things. Just don't forget, you've already got a potential fan club. Treat them like the valuable resource that they are.

Customer service

Customer service is a huge piece of customer retention. Thus, your first mission and most important employee training should reflect excellent customer service.

Your first mission and most important employee training should reflect excellent customer service.

The customer experience cannot be ignored. What is it like from entrance/appointment through purchase/service? Do you have someone to answer the phone during business hours, or do customers have to leave a message to be called back? If they request appointments online, how long until they receive a reply?

The ability to easily collect customer data is priceless. This makes a great resource for you to build an email list. You can use a variety of business software to collect client intake data, create your appointment schedule, send appointment reminders, and follow up with survey requests or send thank-yous. You may hear this software referred to as CRM—customer relationship management. Some CRM software is specific to a given industry, and they can range from simple to very complex. I've seen software that sends a photo of the technician coming to help honor the customer's time (no more four-hour window of wait time) and to help them feel safe by confirming the person at their door is who they say they are. These software programs help you too. You will have fewer no-show appointments when customers receive reminders. However, the cost this incurs needs to be thoughtfully balanced with the benefits it provides you. Bottom line is that the customer experience should feel easy, personal and efficient.

Whether you provide a routine service (like teeth cleanings) or sporadic services (unclogging drains), the potential for customer retention is there. If they visit your office for one massage or one haircut or call you when they overstuffed their washer and need a repair (speaking from experience), you want them to call again next time they need that service, right? Even if you're in the business of providing large services that customers often don't need to do again (pouring concrete for a driveway, remodeling a kitchen or liposuction), you still have an obligation to treat this customer in a way that will make them want to give you repeat business. The customer who needed you to pour new concrete in their driveway might want new concrete poured in their backyard, the new kitchen might need a new bathroom, too, and any kind of body augmentation companies have the opportunity to entice customers to return with additional types of services. Even if they don't call you back for another big service, you want them to recommend you to others. The huge divots in my new driveway ensure that when friends ask for a concrete recommendation, I tell them who *not* to use. Likewise, when I got compliments on my family photos, I raved about the business that took them. Referrals and online reviews can be the heartbeat of your business. Even if a customer may not need your service again, you want to leave them with great things to say about you.

So what do you do about those unhappy customers? I have learned that sometimes in business, you need to "go upside down" to make things right. Meaning if that concrete company had come over and fixed it when we complained about the cracking, I would never have spoken so poorly about them. They may have thought that one customer didn't matter. But I had four friends who had big concrete jobs within six months of mine. That could have been a lot more work for that company. And those four could have told their friends, etc. The news of bad service can travel quickly through social media and review sites, causing lasting damage to your reputation. It's a good idea to have a plan in place when complaints arise.

Sometimes no matter what you do, you lose a customer. But listening to valid complaints and rectifying them can help. Warning, this next paragraph might turn your stomach. You've been warned. At my family's (former) favorite sushi restaurant, we found a hair in my daughter's bento box salad. First time; accidents happen. They apologized and didn't charge us for her meal. So it seemed they had listened to our complaint and took action. We went back a month later. The same thing happened: a long black hair in the salad. I mean honestly, people, have you heard of hairnets? Or ponytails? At this point, it was clear they hadn't really rectified the issue. They had given us a comped meal the first time, but they didn't take action to ensure it wouldn't happen again. Sure, I am just one customer. But I *love* sushi, and I am faithful to my favorites, so now anyone who asks my opinion hears where *not* to go. And chances are if the mistakes kept being made in the same place (the salad), we weren't the only victims. No comped meal could help at that point. Needless to say, we never returned.

KEY TAKEAWAY: Customer care should be a priority in my business.

☐ I will talk to my employees about the importance of customer service. Customer service is important to me because:

5

Marketing Budget

I am the furthest thing from an accountant, but we've got to talk money for a minute. What is your marketing budget? The answer can't be zero. Even if you only do the free marketing tactics, you still have the cost of your time, which is extremely valuable. While you've read marketing options that you can do at no cost, you've read how paid marketing efforts can really boost your customer base and sales. Paid doesn't have to mean expensive. It just has to be done right in order to help you.

Never base your marketing budget on what's left over after covering all other expenses. Likewise, marketing shouldn't be the first thing to go when finances get tight. Putting the brakes on the very thing that can bring you more business is self-sabotage. As the fifth and last child in my family, I really identify with marketing. Everybody puts it last when it's truly the most valuable tool that you can utilize for the success of your business. (And yes, I just called myself the most valuable of the five kids in my family—let's see if any of them read this!)

Consider the cost of *not* marketing your product. If you don't market yourself, how will that affect your bottom line? The costs associated with marketing are really an investment, something that will produce a return over time.

When deciding on your budget, it helps to consider the specific goal you are trying to reach. The local animal shelter runs an advertisement right before their donation campaign in hopes of bringing in more donations. A church runs commercials on the Christian radio station weeks before Christmas in hopes of drawing new families to church. Your goal might simply be to get more customers. But if you're an HVAC company, it might make the most sense to advertise in the late spring as potential customers are gearing up for a hot summer to ensure you get new customers needing HVAC repairs and replacement right away.

Look at the calendar for the next 12 months to get an idea of where and when you'll want to spend your money. If you're ready for a trade show or event booth that's happening this summer, then make sure you've got the money set aside to prepare for that. If you want to try Google Ads, consider what time of year you want that push. Planning ahead will help keep you focused rather than overwhelmed. It's easy to get excited, but I had a client who committed to too much in a short amount of time and then panicked and pulled back on everything. It foiled his plans and caused unnecessary stress. Having a plan will also make you more likely to follow through with and make time for marketing.

According to *Forbes*, it's common for small businesses with revenues less than $5 million to allocate 7–8 percent of their revenues to marketing, splitting that between brand development costs, such as websites, blogs, sales collateral and promotion costs, as well as campaigns, advertising and events. This number may be higher if you're just starting a business because your costs for things like website development will be high while your revenue is still low.

Don't forget to budget the time you spend on marketing as well. While you're learning, your "budget" will need to be higher. But as you develop a routine and feel more comfortable with the strategies, you will have an idea of the appropriate amount of hours that you need to set aside each month.

The best way to set aside this time for myself is to block off hours on my calendar for each specific task. I do this for bookkeeping, too, or else I'd put that off forever. Blocking off time to write social posts or take photos for the website helps hold you accountable and uses your time efficiently. Your social media may be a regularly scheduled timeslot, but you may also want to allocate blocks of time for things like research for advertising, learning your website software, etc. Keeping these regularly scheduled meetings with yourself will help solidify the routine.

KEY TAKEAWAY: I need a marketing budget, even if it only includes the time it takes me to do "free marketing."

☐ I will look at a calendar 6–12 months in advance to help plan the budget for my marketing strategy.

6

Your Company Image

Whoever said that looks don't matter wasn't trying to run a small business. Now that you know what kind of customer you're attracting, how do you create a captivating image that positively portrays your business? Your storefront, vehicles, website, uniforms and even business cards create your image. What does yours say about you?

As you work through this next part, keep the goals and purpose you created in your evaluation in mind. Congratulate yourself on the things you're doing right and consider how improving your image can help you achieve your goals.

Your storefront

Even if you don't have a storefront, you may find pieces that apply, so just sit tight.

When customers approach your storefront, what do they see? Is your building clearly marked with signage that contains your business name? In other words, can people find your business? Is the signage professional? I walked by a storefront in a cute beach town where rent was probably outrageous and businesses were in tough competition to make ends meet. One restaurant had signs made on a home printer with small, hard-to-read font taped sloppily on the windows. Now don't get me wrong, I know that many expenses go into running a business, but when I have 10 restaurants in a two-block radius to choose from, it's not likely that I am going to choose that restaurant. Your signage may make or break whether a customer even walks in. This is a big deal! Your signage should be easy to read, meaning use large print and a readable font. This isn't a place to skimp on the budget. All signage, whether it be the name on the building or etching on the windows, should be professional. Make sure the color you use coordinates with your logo, and keep it simple. You'd never miss a Target you drove by with the splashes of red on their buildings and recognizable bullseye logo, right? They prove that simple is OK. Pay attention to stores the next time you shop. Can you tell what kind of stores they are by the name on the building or the writing on the windows?

Do you know who does a great job of projecting a positive image? Toy stores! I don't even have small children anymore, but give me a colorful window display of cute loveables, books and gadgets, and you'll catch me wandering the aisles for things I didn't even know I needed.

Do you know who can suffer miserably from projecting a poor image? Bakeries. If you're displaying food, be sure it still looks appealing at the end of the day.

Maybe your place of business is an office. The vibe that your office projects can greatly contribute to how your customers feel about you. If it's a doctor's office, are the colors warm, are there magazines to quell nerves, is the noise level calming? If you are a tax preparer, similar principles apply. In addition, potential customers may be judging your trustworthiness. Is the office organized or do you have files everywhere? I once mailed a package at a nearby "business service center." The place gave off the weirdest vibe, and I questioned if they were actually going to mail my package or if the store was just a front for something illegal (blame that on watching too many *Breaking Bad* episodes!). The store had PO boxes where the mail wasn't secure, there were boxes and envelopes sloppily piled in corners, it was dimly lit . . . I could go on, but you're already questioning why I didn't just walk out. Good news, my package *did* get delivered. And maybe just one of those factors wouldn't have given such a bad impression. But multiple fails did not create a good image for the store.

If you don't have a physical location, your image is going to be projected in a different way. For example, I use a well-known pest control company. I have no idea what their offices look like because they come to me. But a decision to use them came from a variety of impressions. I met their employees at a home show where both representatives were dressed professionally in clean, matching company shirts and ironed khaki pants. Their van was wrapped in a design that was easy to read and clearly depicted their company information. They handed me a flyer that helped me understand their products in a clear, concise and accurate format. This impression spoke of professionalism and care for their trade. They were well educated and offered a product I needed at a price I was willing to pay, but I may not have stopped if their signs had been handwritten and their clothes had been sloppy. In opposition was a pest company truck that drove down my street recently. The words "pest control" and a phone number were spelled out with individual sticker letters in a not-so-straight line. I appreciate any effort to make an honest living, but I'm in marketing, and with dozens of companies to choose from, well . . . I'm beginning to sound like a broken record. If you're in the service industry or you deliver to customers, your vehicle is an excellent mode of promotion. Easy-to-read contact information and familiar logos can contribute greatly to your recognizability in the community. It will enhance the impression of professionalism and legitimacy of your business. People need to think that you take your business seriously if you expect them to take you seriously.

People need to think that you take your business seriously if you expect them to take you seriously.

Your website is also a storefront of sorts. We'll talk more about this later, but this is a critical first impression tool if your customers find you through web searches. We've all visited websites that load slowly, have too many pop-ups or are missing critical information. We're going to make sure that isn't you!

Marketing materials

If they are done well, business cards, flyers, car wraps and other marketing materials can be very helpful tools for your business.

Basic must-haves:

•a logo and/or your business name that is printed in a font that never changes

•fonts and color schemes that match/complement each other on all of your material

This regularity creates recognizability when customers repeatedly see your logo or business name. Your letterhead, cards, brochures, etc. should all have the feeling that they go together.

You don't need to spend a fortune to make them look professional, and the return in credibility is priceless. I met a woman who was trying to get hired as a contractor with a company I was working for. She bragged about her résumé, telling me in not-so-subtle ways how much of an asset she would be. "Here is my card," she told me. "I'm not cheap, but if I can fit it into my schedule, I can work for you." As I was already forming my opinion about her humble personality, I looked at the card. "Oh, my number changed but I never printed new ones. I just scratched it out and wrote my new one down." Friends, this card was glossy, so the scratches from the ink pen made the new number hard to read and so sloppy. This woman just spent 10 minutes telling me how skilled and sought-after she was, but she can't spring for the $25 it costs to print new cards? This might not always kill a deal, but it will never leave a great impression.

You may not be artistic, and that's OK. Being all things as a small business owner is impossible. But you can find plenty of resources. There are free programs online like canva.com that will help you design marketing material. Also, businesses like Staples have templates online to help your material look professional. Still, something you don't want to deal with? Hire someone. More about hiring someone later.

Employees

Depending on your business, the dress code may vary considerably. But I think it's accurate to assume that everyone wants their employees to be safe, be clean and offer great customer service. If employees wear company shirts, they should be clean, fit appropriately and not have holes. Shoes should be job appropriate. Hair should be neat. All of these guidelines apply whether you're a tattoo artist, barista or a repair person. These things may seem like no-brainers, but it's better to spell out your expectations than be surprised. When every member of your team understands the value of the customer—who essentially signs their paychecks—it should be easier to get them on board with being part of your business's image.

Exercise: How is your image?

(You can download this question worksheet at thejenadvantage.com.)

Answer these questions to assess your image:

Storefront

•Is it clean (inside and out)?

•Is your business name clearly visible?

•Is other pertinent information (hours, contact info, etc.) posted and professional?

•Do your displays look appealing?

•Is the vibe inviting?

•Considering what you've read, how can you improve your storefront?

Alternate "storefront"

•Do your company vehicles look professional?

•Are your vehicles clearly marked with your company information?

•Do you have a website? Is it user-friendly?

•Is the messaging clear?

Marketing materials

•Do you have business cards, brochures, car wraps?

•Do they all match?

•Is the information clear and correct?

•Is it easy to read (color, font, font size)?

Employees

•Do they know your expectations on dress code?

•Do you have a customer service policy?

KEY TAKEAWAY: The image of my business greatly contributes to how customers perceive me.

☐ One thing I'm doing really great is:

If you are like most small business owners that I talk to, you barely have time to breathe let alone the time to take a magnifying glass to your business. But I hope you have seen the benefit of it whether you are just starting out or you've been in business for a while. Have your answers surprised you? Disappointed you? Excited you? I wish we could chat about it! While I am happy that I will be able to help more small businesses by writing this book, perhaps the biggest drawback is the lack of personal connection because I am dying to know right now what you think so far. Now that you've evaluated your business, you may be able to clearly see the areas that need advancement in order to make your dreams a reality. No doubt marketing will have something to do with achieving these goals. So let's get to the real reason you came to this party!

Part 2

Marketing

Wahoo! Time for the fun stuff—marketing! OK, I realize that if this were the fun part for you, you probably wouldn't need this book. But I am going to break this down and simplify it as much as possible so it can make sense to you and so you can make an educated decision about what is going to work best for your business. If you completed the tasks in the first few chapters, you should have a pretty solid idea of your business, who you are and what makes your business special. In addition, you've set some goals that will help you focus on the direction you're going to go.

Before we start can we agree on something? I really only have one rule. It's my golden rule. In marketing, your information needs to be accurate. Integrity and authenticity are the building blocks of my business, and they should be yours too.

Integrity and authenticity are the building blocks of my business, and they should be yours too.

Why? Because the American public has been lied to so much that they don't trust anything they hear. When your audience is filled with skeptics, you have no other choice but to be honest. Even unintentional errors can hamper your reputation. Outdated websites, broken links and expired coupons or inaccurate pricing can cause questions about your reliability. The temptation to cut corners and choose "easy" instead of "right" can be hard to battle. But your success with marketing relies on honest messaging. Period.

Something else you should know: this part of the book is going to touch on dozens of ways to market your business, but don't try to do them all at once! You will overwhelm yourself, and frankly, it's not necessary. As you read, mark what you like and note what sounds like it might work for you. We'll create a plan in the last section.

Before we dive in, keep a few things in mind.

Marketing is a process, not an event.

Patience—I hope you were blessed with more of it than I was. But building your customer base through marketing takes time. A quick internet search will yield all sorts of theories about how many impressions it takes to make a sale. A good average for the purpose of this book is eight. So, what does that mean to you? It means it takes eight impressions before somebody decides to use your business. How do I know and what does this mean? Take the new restaurant that just opened across town from me.

Impression One: I had coffee in the shopping center as they were preparing for it to open.

Two: I told my husband where it was, and he confirmed he heard that the area was finally getting some new businesses.

Three: I had seen friends post on social media about going there—the food looked good!

Four: I got a gift card for Christmas for the restaurant.

Five: My niece found out about the gift card and told me to call her before we went—they go there all the time.

Six: I drove by the restaurant last week and was reminded I still have that gift card . . .

Seven: The local chamber of commerce highlights a restaurant each week, and they were this week's highlight.

Friends, I still haven't gone. I have this gift card, so obviously, I will, but I still haven't. Why not? Everything about it that I've heard is great. The food sounds amazing, the cocktails look delicious and the restaurant is aesthetic. All positive signs, and I still haven't gone. So in the restaurant business, perhaps it takes more than eight impressions? In my marketing business, I have found it actually only takes about four impressions before I start working with a client.

Regardless of the number of impressions needed, the goal is to make impressions in different places to ensure you're reaching your potential customers. If you only do radio advertising, you might completely miss your demographic who only streams music. Relying 100 percent on Facebook ads isn't going to help you reach people without social media (yes, they exist, my husband for example). While my advice will always be to start small, I definitely encourage you to try different approaches to get the word out.

A handyman posted signs around my neighborhood, and then later that month, I saw the company truck drive by. A few weeks after, I heard a commercial for him on the radio. Each impression alone wasn't enough to make a huge impact, but the three consecutive impressions legitimized his business for me. Personally, my next step will be to read reviews since the commercial said he had over 100 five-star reviews. In this case, it may have only taken him four impressions to get business.

Bottom line is that it's not an exact science. So don't stress over the number of impressions; just know that multiple impressions are a thing and you need to make them in multiple places.

It also really depends on the business you're in. What works for a hairstylist might not necessarily work for a restaurant. The messaging has to be different due to different motivations to make a purchase. This means that a bed and breakfast might find a lot of success with social media image ads, whereas the stylist might find the most success with a video ad on YouTube. How do you know which is best?

Time and a little trial and error. Be patient, monitor your metrics and adjust based on that data. If one channel appears to be working better than another, go bananas! But I can't tell you how many times I've talked to a client who wonders why business isn't booming after a week of running one ad. That's just not the way it works. It takes time for messages to sink in, and a consumer has to be ready for your product. Consistency is the name of the game. Remember the old story of the tortoise and the hare? Be the tortoise.

Creating consistent messaging across multiple platforms to make these impressions is referred to as *integrated marketing*. This means using the same visual elements and unified messaging so that a customer is more likely to recognize (and remember!) your company when they see an online ad that has the same color scheme and wording as your company van they saw driving through town. Customers appreciate the predictability and consistency that this integrated messaging creates. Keep this in mind with everything from business cards to website design to employee uniforms.

As we go through the different types of marketing, keep in mind how yours compares to the standard. Are you exceeding, or do you need help? Will the marketing tactic help you reach your goal? Use the space provided to note if you're exceeding or need help in a given marketing area (social media, print, radio, online, etc.), and be sure to note which strategy is relevant to your business and helps achieve your goals.

Free marketing

We're going to begin with resources for free marketing. Keep in mind free doesn't mean better (or not valuable); it's just a great place to start if you have budget constraints. But everything takes time, and your time is valuable, so whether free or paid, keep in mind how your time and bank account are affected.

Online Reviews and Referrals

If you think that you have no control over how your online reviews and word-of-mouth referrals affect your marketing, please revisit the section on customer service. The goal after each loan closed, coffee served or bike purchased is to give them only good things to say about you.

The goal after each loan closed, coffee served or bike purchased is to give them only good things to say about you.

If you're not asking your customers to leave you online reviews, you aren't capitalizing on all your effort toward providing excellent service. It's because of that excellent service that they want to help you!

Why do I need to?

Everyone has an opinion these days, and they love to share it with others. Did you know that 97 percent of customers consult reviews? Did you know that positive reviews boost your search engine optimization (SEO)? Online customer reviews gain more weight in organic local searches (translation: your business shows up in searches more often when someone is searching for a company in your industry). Hearing feedback on what is working and where you need help is also useful to you.

You want to use online review websites to give your customers an easy platform to share their great experiences, and in turn, your future customers can go there to read about it.

But what if the reviews are bad?

I was once told by a business owner that they didn't want to mess with online reviews or "claiming their page" on Yelp because they had heard it's impossible to get rid of the bad reviews, and those could be really bad for business.

Hmm. Maybe you're thinking what I was: What if you run your business in such a way that you aren't worried about bad reviews? I mean, he's not wrong that it *is* impossible to get rid of the bad reviews. And full disclosure: you'll probably get some. You will miss an appointment, your service won't be up to a customer's standard, or someone will just have a grumpy disposition and can't be pleased. But the good reviews will overshadow the bad. Give consumers the benefit of the doubt that they can weed out the complainers over truly negative experiences. For example, I got a kick out of this review for a well-established coffee house with an excellent reputation: The reviewer stated that her visit was going well, and she was enjoying her drink until . . . "[she] saw a staff member going around wiping down tables but he seemed to skip [hers] since [she] was sitting there. Maybe management can remind staff to ask customers if they would like their table wiped down.

[Her] table was actually a bit dusty and could have used it."

Really? This gave them a three-star rating? My lord. You know, she could have spoken up and asked the staff to wipe her table. Business owners: your job is not easy. I see you! OK, done with my rant and back to business here.

I'm going to assume that if you're investing this time into your business, you run a place where you're doing your best to earn good reviews, so when the bad reviews come, they won't hurt you. Customers find a mix of positive and negative reviews more trustworthy, so don't stress too much.

Which sites to use

There are a lot of sites across the internet where people can leave reviews. I recommend just choosing a couple of the more popular ones to focus on. Just because there are 45 sites where you could create a profile and glean reviews does not mean that you should. Most people gravitate toward sites like Yelp and Google reviews. Customers looking for referrals from their friends and neighbors may also gravitate to sites like Nextdoor and Facebook.

Be aware that there are paid features on these sites, and some can inundate you with emails about why you should use their paid services. It's important to know that you do not have to pay to use their site.

What to include in your profile

After you select which sites to use, take the time to complete your profile. Many profiles, like the ones on Yelp, allow you to upload pictures. Make sure these images are high resolution (they don't look blurry). You could upload photos of your logo, your team, the interior/exterior of your business, employees "in action" or products that you offer. If you upload coupons or special offers, be sure you take them down when they expire. I was just looking at a new client's page, and it had a coupon that expired three years ago. I know he's busy, and it is so hard to do it all. My advice would be if you're strapped on time, only include "timeless" photos and not offers with dates that you have to keep track of.

Yelp also allows you to include highlights, like veteran owned or in business for 20 years. Use whatever applies to you! You'll be able to list the services you offer and write a description of the business. Be sure this reflects you well. This is going to be your first impression for many potential customers. If you're using multiple review sites like Yelp and Google, be sure that you're using the same information on each one for continuity and recognizability.

Keep track of your usernames and passwords. It's important to keep your information up-to-date across all platforms. If your location or hours change, you need to keep that updated. Fresh photos every few months are a good idea too.

How to get customers to leave reviews

When your service is complete, you should ask your customers to leave a review. Even better, snap a picture with the happy customer and post it to your social channels (with permission, of course). Testimonials are a goldmine, and showing the relationships you've built through photos tells the story of your consistent reliability. Done with a haircut? Review, please! Beautiful flower arrangement sent to Mom? Review, please! Home loan funded? Yes, you got it, review, please! You can do this in various ways. Whichever way you make the ask, it needs to be as easy as possible to get the customer to take the time:

•In person is the first option, albeit the most direct, and therefore, your employees may not love this part of the job.

•If you are offering counter service, you can put a QR code on the counter or on the receipt that goes straight to Google reviews.

•If you send invoices, include the link to the review website.

•Do you collect your customers' emails? (Psst. You should!) Send a follow-up email after service with direct links to review you.

You're not bothering them. This is customary. I have seen companies do promotions to build their reviews like save $1 on your next ice cream when you write a review. However, this can be a daunting task to keep track of and questionably unethical if it seems that you are "paying" for reviews. Be sure you know the policies of the review sites you are using. You're smart. I trust your decisions.

Interact with customers

Once those reviews start rolling in, interact with your customers. A simple thank-you goes a long way. The customer feels appreciated and future consumers see that you're attentive. If the review was less than favorable, this is not the place to have the discussion to fix the problem. A response apologizing for their unhappiness and promising to contact them (or offering your email for them to reach you) still shows your concern without airing the details all over the internet. You can always respond to a review to show the customers that you care and provide additional context.

Utilize these reviews

All of these positive reviews that you're collecting don't just have to live on the site where your customer wrote the referral. Use reviews on your website to help promote your products. Your website can point to the review sites so they can see all of your reviews or write their own. Reviews are great to use in social posts or on brochures. Somebody thinks you're great—let the whole world know!

KEY TAKEAWAY: Reviews are a free and easy way to build trust in consumers.

☐ I will ask satisfied customers to write reviews about my business.

8

Google Business Profile

Google has many paid advertising options, but a Google Business Profile is free. By creating one, you can manage how your business appears in Google searches and maps to help customers find you. You can include:

•information about your services, location, hours of operation and special holiday hours

•photos of your work

•posts about your latest news

•posts about an upcoming sale

You can also monitor the performance metrics of your profile. You'll be able to see how many people searched for your site, viewed your profile, called your business, sought directions to your business and so much more. It's important to have accurate information about your business easily available to your customers.

Creating a Google Business Profile is simple and doesn't take much time. The dashboard of your profile is easy to navigate. From here you can copy a direct link to ask customers to write a review. You must have a verified Google Business Profile to respond to reviews that customers leave for you. Responding to reviews builds trust and shows your appreciation for customers' time. Why care about Google reviews? Because people check Google reviews more than any other review site. Those reviews, good and bad, have a direct correlation with where you appear in the search ranking.

Once you've got it set up, be sure you refresh your photos and posts every once in a while to keep it looking up-to-date.

KEY TAKEAWAY: My Google Business Profile helps customers find my business and enables them to leave reviews.

□ I will set up and/or update my Google Business Profile.

Free Options in Traditional Media

Maybe you remember the days when we only got our news from the daily newspaper and the 11 o'clock news. While the smartphone and desktop computer give us access to overwhelming amounts of information, do not overlook good ol'-fashioned media. When establishing your business, the key is to know your audience and meet them where they're at. Also, keep in mind that anytime your business name appears in print, it helps with your SEO.

Television, radio or podcast

Many cities have local morning shows whose main purpose is to highlight local causes, businesses, events, etc. If this exists in your area, take advantage of them! I had a landscape designer tell me how her phone didn't stop ringing the afternoon that she did a short spot about her favorite plants to put in a spring garden. These programs are always looking for new content.

When pitching your idea, remember that it's always about your customer's problem. While you and I both know that you want to appear on their show to get more customers and build your business, that isn't going to get you hired. Be sure to frame your ask for time on the air with how you can help their viewers. While it's wise to have your topic ready to pitch, be flexible if they ask you to cover something a little different. So long as it pertains to your industry and you can still gain business from it, getting a yes is a win.

Once you get the green light, ask questions so you know exactly what to expect:

•What time do you need to arrive?

•Will you be on a set?

•Is there space for you to bring props (if you need them)?

•Who will be interviewing you?

•How long will you have on air?

My question to you is this: Are you the best person in your company to go on air? Not everyone has the attributes for speaking to an audience or on camera, and that's OK! If you have an employee whose strength is being a charismatic communicator, maybe they're a better choice to represent your company. Once that's decided, rehearse. Usually, the questions and topic will be decided in advance so you'll know what to practice. If you want to offer a special for viewers if they order/book/purchase by a certain date, be sure the TV hosts have that information. You don't want to sound like a recording, so practice being natural and conversational. Have somebody practice with you to get feedback.

On the day of, be sure that your appearance is clean and polished. If applicable, wear your company logo. Do *not* wear the company sweatshirt that is your favorite with holes and bleach stains. This is your time to shine! Be sure to bring any cards or flyers to leave for their staff. Even a coupon for a service is a nice gesture. Relax, have fun and be prepared for some phone calls!

Don't have a local television show? What about a local radio show? That might be an avenue for you to explore too. If you are a car mechanic and there is a local radio show for car fanatics, you might just have the expertise they are looking for. Is radio too old-school for you? Am I dating myself? OK, fine, how about a podcast? While podcasts can be nationwide, if your business is brick-and-mortar or just servicing a local area, you want to find a podcast with a local audience. But depending on your industry and area of expertise, it could be just what you're looking for.

Local magazine and newspaper or blog coverage

When I started my business and had to file a "doing business as" with my county, I remember thinking how antiquated it was that they still make people run an ad in the newspaper for it. I wondered if that's what was keeping these dear newspapers alive. And this is coming from someone with a journalism degree, so I'm allowed to rag on my old industry. But, regardless of the decline in subscription sales, newspapers are still very much a thing, and with an online presence, they are an authoritative source to have your business featured in.

Similar to the TV appearance, you need an idea to pitch to them to make them want to write about you. The article may not even focus on what your business does. I have a client who pays for the adoption of a cat each month and has rescued over 40 cats. That article may be the perfect human interest story they are looking for, but of course, the article would mention and give credit to the company name. Partnering with the organizations where you do philanthropy is a great press opportunity.

Other print resources are local magazines and local blog coverage. Research your area and learn what your options are. Everybody needs content. You just need to have a good enough pitch to make them want yours.

You can lighten the load of the reporter and write the story for them. Press releases work well if you're offering a new service. Maybe you've merged with another company, or your company has been recognized with an award. Maybe the press release announces the new partnership between you and a charitable organization. Instead of blasting every media-related email address you can find, I recommend doing a bit of legwork and sending a personal note to journalists who already write about business or your field. It's more likely to be taken seriously instead of considered spam mail. Press releases are still relevant and an excellent way to earn free media coverage. Earned media coverage (coverage you didn't pay for) can be so powerful because it adds to your credibility as an authority on the subject and leverages the media outlet's audience as you're trying to build yours.

Getting published

Publishing articles for trade journals, websites about your field, etc. helps support that you're an authority in your field. Ask yourself what problems you solve and what you can educate people about. Now think about which publications would want this information. You can really elevate your business by creating a partnership. If you're a personal trainer, think about health stores or workout apparel companies. Or maybe you're a veterinarian partnering with a pet food store. You can write articles for them that can also be posted to your social media sites and add content to your website. It confirms to readers/potential clients that you're a trusted authority. It gives you recognition that this media outlet published your work. If your business is online/nationwide, this can really help you spread your reach.

What subject are you an authority on? What expertise can you offer others in your field? What problems can you solve for people? Think about these things and then consider what sources would want to publish you. Are you a member of a local trade organization? Are there magazines or blogs for your trade? Find your resources and refine your pitch.

KEY TAKEAWAY: Traditional media is not to be overlooked when creating my marketing strategy.

☐ I will brainstorm ways that traditional media marketing can work for my business.

10

All Things Social Media

Social media—you either love it or you hate it. But it's here to stay, and it's an excellent way to reach customers. Before you get overwhelmed, let me assure you that you don't need a presence on every platform. They won't all be useful to you. It's better to do a few things really well than stretch yourself so thin that you fail at everything.

Social media serves you in multiple ways. You can:

•reach people on their phone, which most people never let out of their sight

•drive traffic to your website

•glean insight into the demographics of your audience

•build brand loyalty

•keep an eye on what your competitors are doing

•collect emails through a contest

•pay attention to your insights and change your strategies if needed

If your followers see you being active and responsive, they're much more likely to do business with you than a company with no social media presence or a poorly run page.

The evolution of social media seems to be that it becomes cool with the teenagers, and then parents jump on board to try it out. Facebook was for the youngins until Mom and Dad (and Grandma) found it a great place to keep up with old classmates and follow their favorite Etsy creator, so the youth left it for Instagram. Kids posted their selfies, watched how many "likes" each selfie received and celebrated when it hit over 100. Adults followed behind, posting and sharing positive quotes, political memes and the highlight reels from their family vacation. The youth jumped ship and quickly swam to Snapchat, where they currently reside. But not to leave out that while the youth love YouTube, Mom and Dad have infiltrated that website as well. Content is still heavily created for all ages on YouTube, but to accommodate the fact that children's attention span is about 10 seconds, TikTok entered the arena to meet that need. Then there is Twitter. An animal of its own, Twitter is a platform for people who have a lot to say. The emergence of competing platforms is on the rise, trying to meet the need of a population looking for less censorship. Even between writing this and being published, a new platform may emerge. If anything is guaranteed with social media, it's change.

For businesses who rely on social media advertising, this means they need to keep up with their audience and shift platforms when demographics move. That doesn't mean a company completely leaves one platform for another; it just means the content on each platform may be geared toward a different demographic. For example, with the theater I mentioned—their audience was their students, parents and patrons—the parents and patrons primarily interact on Facebook, while almost all student interaction is done on Instagram, so they put out content on both platforms. They often use the same content but gear the messaging to hit the right crowd. If they want to be sure kids know about a special event like a skate night or auditions, they make sure that goes on Instagram. They share the students posts when they tag the theater and create fun quizzes to keep that age group engaged. If they want to sell tickets to a show, that is pushed on Facebook, where more of their patrons follow along.

Are you wondering which platform you're best suited for? Let's chat about your options. I'm going to give you:

•an overview of the most popular (to date) platforms

•some statistics that support the information

•"bottom line" takeaways

You know your attention span. For all the skimmers out there, you're welcome.

Which platform(s) should I use?

You've already done the exercise to determine your target audience and to know if it's small and focused or really broad. Keep that information in mind as you read through the different platforms to decide what you think will work for you. If you're still stumped, do a survey! Ask your customers about their social media use. Where do they have accounts? Where do they do most of their interacting? Spend one month where every employee asks the clients this question. It can give you a great starting point when planning your social media strategy. You could even give them a pen or other small promotional item with your logo as a thank-you if you feel inclined, but most customers will gladly help without an incentive.

Facebook

Overview: Facebook allows users to set up profiles and connect with friends and businesses online. Many users follow news networks, getting their news primarily on Facebook. Many follow celebrities and use the website as their insight into entertainment, sports and politics. And then other users are part of groups that connect them to like-minded individuals. Users can share photos, videos and, of course, their opinion.

Facebook is easy to use, and its Meta Business Suite tool makes creating posts very easy. They provide great insight tools to monitor your metrics and many advertising options. They even have a planning calendar to help you schedule your posts.

These stats below show you the sheer impact that Facebook has on humans. You don't need to remember these numbers; you just need to read them to remember why you're spending time on social media.

Stats:

•There are almost 3 billion Facebook users and almost 2 billion are active daily. (For comparison, there are 7 billion people in the world and 2.9 do not have internet access.)

•6 out of 10 adults in the US have an account, with 73 percent accessing it daily and 93 percent using it weekly.

•Facebook has a fairly even spread across demographics. The senior population is the smallest; however, it's the only platform that has a significant senior presence. Even though 24 percent of Facebook's audience are people ages 18–24, you can reach that age group on all of the other platforms as well.

Bottom line: If you're on any social media, this is probably where you need to be. It has the largest reach and broadest demographic.

Instagram

Overview: While other platforms put emphasis on words, Instagram is largely image/video driven. Users connect here to not only follow their friends but also celebrities and product influencers, whose images help shape the way they are informed about styles, products and news that they are interested in. Instagram offers special features for business accounts, all free to use (with the exception of ads, of course). It has gone through some growing pains and has never seemed to quite solve the problem of getting a bigger reach. But don't let that deter you.

Something to note is that this platform was created for smartphones, so it offers very limited interactions on a desktop computer.

Because Instagram is owned by Facebook, they've made it very easy to post your content in both places at once. Your content may not always be relevant in both places, though. For example, you can't put links in the text descriptions on Instagram. However, with ease of use, it's a no-brainer to post your content in both places.

Instagram has other features like "stories," where images posted expire after 24 hours, and the ability to post videos and share posts from others. This helps create a highly interactive experience, which makes it no wonder that users spend almost an hour on it per day.

Stats:

•There are over one billion users worldwide.

•Over two-thirds of users are under 35 and users spend an average of 53 minutes on the site each day.

Bottom line: Instagram is image driven. Take the time to capture quality images/videos to capture the user's attention.

YouTube

Overview: To put it simply, YouTube is a video-sharing service. Video captures a message in a way that a photo simply cannot. Our attention span is waning, so video is an excellent way to combat that. And while social platforms have the option to post videos, YouTube is unique. Unlike social sites where users are scrolling without intent, when people go to YouTube, they have a purpose in mind. It's not just Fortnite videos they're watching or the YouTube sensation Mila. They want to find you. A large reason for this is that many individuals simply prefer to watch a video than read an article.

An added benefit of posting video content to YouTube is its syndication. YouTube isn't the end destination of your content; it's just the beginning. YouTube makes it extremely easy for your content to be shared with others through other channels like Facebook, Twitter, LinkedIn, email and other websites.

Stats:

•With over two billion users, YouTube is the second largest search engine next to Google. This statistic is staggering. That means that besides Google, YouTube is the most popular place for people to search the internet.

•Videos make things easier to understand. Viewers retain 95 percent when they watch a video compared to 10 percent when reading it in text. This explains the plethora of "how-to" videos and guides designed to teach viewers everything from changing the oil in a car to cooking the perfect omelet.

• 72 percent of customers would rather learn about a product or service by way of video than alternatives like text or infographics.

•Because video is so effective, it often gets shared by the individual who watched it. In fact, videos generate 1,200 percent more shares than images and text combined.

Bottom line: Many of your customers prefer video, so give them what they want. If you're camera shy, now might be the time to get over it. Or find someone on your team to take the reins. Your customers are already there, so go meet them!

Twitter

Overview: Twitter is a social network that connects people sharing their thoughts. "Tweets" are sound bites and conversations that are happening in real-time, so unless you have time to be engaging throughout the day, this may not be the platform for you. Before deciding on using Twitter, ask yourself if your industry peers are using it with success. Does it make sense for your business?

Because of the time-sensitive nature, this is not a platform where most small businesses are going to want to use their resources.

Stats:

•With just over two million daily active users, the Twitter population pales in comparison to its other social buddies.

•99 percent of Twitter users also use at least one other social media network.

Bottom line: Unless this really makes sense for your industry, this is probably a platform that you can skip for now.

TikTok, Snapchat, Whatchamacallit

You're correct if you find yourself thinking that you've never heard of Whatchamacallit. Don't bother checking the app store—it's not a social platform, yet. I only mean to say that along with TikTok and Snapchat, other social tools are available and emerging.

Should you be using them? That depends. How much time do you really have to devote to this? Developing, posting and responding to content takes time, and preparing it for multiple sites amplifies that time. Videos take a little more time and creativity. That said, if you're an avid TikTok user and making videos comes naturally to you, use it if it makes sense for your business! TikTok has roughly the same user statistics as Instagram. However, 30 percent of their users are under the age of 19. If you're selling air conditioners, that probably isn't helpful. If you're selling donuts, sports gear or anything kid related, then this could be your place.

Snapchat, like Twitter, is time-consuming. If you're already a user, you may want to try it for your business. It's definitely not a platform to dive into for the sporadic social media user, though.

As for any other platforms I missed or that are yet to emerge, do what makes sense. Some social sites are specific to industries, so if that pertains to you, explore them.

Start small with content for one or two platforms. But remember that social media is only one piece of a large puzzle. If this is outside of your comfort zone, you're going to need to bend a little to do the bare minimum. If this is your wheelhouse, you may need to be careful that you don't pour so much effort into it that you forget the other critical pieces of your marketing plan.

If this is outside of your comfort zone, you're going to need to bend a little to do the bare minimum.

Create and grow your social media

You may already use social media, but I hope you've given discerning thought to what is right for your business. Even if you're already a user, it's always good to revisit your practices to get rid of what doesn't work and build upon what does.

The next steps primarily relate to Facebook and Instagram, though pieces relate to all platforms. We'll touch on YouTube too!

Next steps:

•create your profile

•invite followers

•create your content calendar

•create the content

Your profile

Once you've chosen social networks to focus on, you need to create a profile. Each platform varies, but the basics you'll need to include are a profile photo, name and description of your business. Be sure the photo is high quality (the image doesn't look grainy or blurry) and is a clear depiction of your business. This might be your logo, company name, product image or team photo.

Be detailed in your description. You could say, "carpet cleaner," but you could also say, "Family-owned carpet cleaning specializing in eco-conscious products. Guaranteed to remove any stain or your money back. Serving the Sacramento area." Which do you think encourages a customer to reach out? If you need ideas, look at other businesses in your industry. They say imitation is the best form of flattery, right? Also, don't forget to include a link to your website and contact info. The more complete the information, the better chance people can find you.

What you need:

•business name

•page "username" (if applicable)

•clear and professional photo

•business description

•website link

•contact information

•the area you serve (don't limit just to the town you're in if it makes sense to also include surrounding cities)

•any additional information you'd like to include

Followers

Getting followers will take some time. You can start by inviting your friends to follow you. Facebook makes this super easy with the click of a button. You can make some of your staff "admins" on the page and ask them to invite their friends too.

Funnel your followers on other channels to like or follow your new page. This could be tweeting out your Facebook URL or sending an email to all your customers with a link to the new social page. Make it as easy as possible. Put your social links in your email signature and create a QR code (easy to do on canva.com!) to your social pages, then put that on your business card or flyers.

Include "follow us" messaging in all of your communication. This means invoices, emails, flyers, signs at the register or anywhere else that seems a natural fit. Create the habit of asking your customers to follow your page. If this is not your strength, try this:

You: We're on Facebook and Instagram, do you follow us yet?

Them: No, I don't.

You: It's a great way to learn about everything we offer and to make sure you don't miss a special.

Them: OK. (But are they going to do it? Keep the conversation going.)

You: Do you prefer Facebook or Instagram?

Them: I spend the most time on Instagram.

You: OK, well then just look for (your username), and you'll find us there. We have some specials coming up soon, and this way you don't miss them.

Simple, right? Keep it brief and light. This is something all of your staff should be trained on. Of course, you don't want to make it weird or awkward. It may not be fitting for every customer. Practice scenarios with your staff and get them comfortable with making the ask. They need to know how to ask for reviews, so this can be included in that training.

Last, on sites like Twitter or Instagram, make sure your business page is following others. When you follow products you use, members in your chamber of commerce or any other relevant people/companies will be inclined to follow you back. The liking and sharing help immensely with your growth.

Posting to your social accounts

So you've got your account set up and you've got some followers. Time to start posting! Unfortunately, this is where a lot of people get stuck. But you're reading this book so that won't be you! What you post and when you post it matters.

I highly recommend that you plan your social posts in advance. Planning your posts in advance takes a bit of time up front, but once it's done, you don't have to think about it again. It's actually much easier to create a handful at a time because once the creativity starts flowing, it's easier to keep going. If you are used to posting when the mood strikes, you could go days, weeks or even months between posts. But by planning, you ensure consistency, which is what your customers need. Remember, they need multiple impressions to remember and use your company. Consistently posting is a great way to start.

Every business is different, but for the sake of the book, I am going to assume you don't have a full-time marketing manager. That means either you or an employee will be doing the posts in addition to your or their regular job. That's why we're planning in advance. Usually, one month in advance is great, but some industries may need to be done in two-week intervals. A great place to start is planning 12 posts per month. That's almost every other day. Feel free to come up with more, but before you spend more time on this, begin to measure the results of the 12.

If at any time this feels unnecessary or you're tempted to put it off, you've got to remember that consistency is key. If you haven't posted for three months, a potential customer who visits your page may question if you are still in business. If your page shows you on again/off again with posting, a customer may question your reliability. But that won't be you because we're going to craft those regular posts next. Let's brainstorm!

Post topics

This is my favorite part! The possibilities are endless. Let's have a brainstorming session and help you collect your thoughts. You can do this on a blank sheet of paper or download the worksheet on my website.

If you don't have the worksheet, draw six equal boxes on the paper.

BOX 1: Your business. What is your business? What kind of products or services do you offer? This isn't just "I'm a hairstylist." It's cut, color, shampoo, wedding/prom style, extensions, etc. This isn't "I'm an HVAC company." It's service calls, troubleshooting, maintenance, filter change, new product installation, offer rebates, install whole-house fans, repair and replace ductwork, etc. Details matter! Go back to the business evaluation if you need help with this. We're putting it all here so we don't forget all of the things we have to tell our customers about.

BOX 2: Your interests. Do you love coffee, ice cream or pizza? Do you play a recreational sport? Are you crazy about cats? Do you love watching college football? Does one of your employees have a cool talent, like maybe they're in a band? Or it could be as simple as being left-handed (because that is almost a superpower, just saying). Whatever it is, it goes in this box.

BOX 3: Employees. If you're a small company, write their individual names. If you have a lot of employees or seasonal turnover, just write their main duties (technician, office admin, cashier, etc.).

BOX 4: Events you participate in/philanthropy. Are you registered to have a booth at a local event? Are you sponsoring an industry event? Do you donate or volunteer for a nonprofit? Is there an annual conference you attend? All those things go in this box.

BOX 5: Partner companies. Are you brand loyal, meaning all your tools or products are the same brand? What are those brands? Do you have partners in your industry? Do you have other partners, like a restaurant where you always hold your team meetings, or other businesses you use to support yours, like a printing shop, uniform shop, supply store, etc.? Write them here.

BOX 6: Holidays and special days. Holidays like Christmas might be a no-brainer, but are there other holidays that you want to be sure to honor? Do you give military discounts (Veterans Day), do you want to wish moms a happy Mother's Day, does your business have an anniversary sale, etc.? Also, there are hundreds of "national day of" celebrations. I've included a list of my favorites in the downloadable worksheets, but a simple internet search will show you what I mean. Can I hear it for National Taco Day? It's October 4, in case you want to write that one down.

Keep this list handy when planning your posts. It will help you create well-rounded posts without repeating topics too often. Most businesses can plan their posts two–four weeks ahead. I prefer a month ahead, but experiment to see what works for you. It takes a bit of time to do it all at once, but then you don't have to remember to do it again for a month!

To do this, begin by looking at the month and referring to your BOX 6 to see if there are any holidays or special events that you want to acknowledge. Mark those days. Next, check your calendar against BOX 4 and check for the same thing. Is the dog shelter you support holding a gala? Are you speaking at a conference? Mark those days for a post. In reference to your hobby/likes list (BOX 2), you can search for relevant "national day of" holidays to post about. Did you know that National Ice Cream Day is always the third Sunday in July? Are you left-handed like me? Southpaws are celebrated on August 13 each year. Choose your favorites to include in your posting schedule.

I didn't forget that you actually have a business to post about. Filling in the space around the days you've marked, next refer to BOX 1. Choose a few of your services to highlight. Referring to BOX 3, how can you highlight your employees? You could pick one a month to highlight. Maybe there is a national day for their trade, or you want to highlight their awesome teamwork. Whichever way you incorporate it, be sure they get a shout-out. It's a great morale booster. Other topics to consider posting about are your online reviews and asking customers to leave a review about their experience. Before and after photos are also a great way to showcase your work. Shocking (honest) statistics are sure to grab attention.

Keep in mind that consumers like interaction. So do the occasional quiz or poll in your stories to attract engagement. You should also make it a habit to share others' posts on occasion. When that nonprofit announces their gala, when your favorite tool brand is having a sale, when your business card printer is having a sale—SHARE. You want people to do the same for you, so it's only right to share the love.

Sharing posts that have anything to do with BOX 2, 4 or 5:

•BOX 2: Love golf? Share the latest post from your favorite golf course. Is your employee's band playing this weekend? Share that post.

•BOX 4: Did registration just open up for an event you're sponsoring? Share the post.

•BOX 5: Is something cool going on at one of your partner companies? Let your followers know by sharing it!

Here is what a sample calendar looks like for an electrician client.

September

Sept. 1 Labor Day post (family pic at lake, hope everyone is having a good weekend)
Sept. 4 Employee highlight
Sept. 5 EV charger—video on-site at install
Sept. 9 Solar panels
Sept. 11 In honor of 9/11
Sept. 13 Happy 25th anniversary to the owners
Sept. 16 Recent review—ask for reviews
Sept. 18 Team photos of volunteering at creek cleanup
Sept. 21 Basic electrical work
Sept. 24 New product alert (tag product company)
Sept. 25 Link to monthly newsletter
Sept. 28 Team meeting at coffee shop (tag coffee shop)

While you can schedule all of these ahead of time, it's important to monitor your social media in case you get comments or in case your partners have posts that you want to share. We're just creating a base for you to ensure the consistency that I keep talking about, but you can have fun with this!

With either the downloaded calendar or your own, choose a month to plan posts for.

Keep in mind that I suggest you start with 12 posts per month. Yes, you can do more, but I want you to start with a manageable number that still encourages good engagement. There is no hard-and-fast rule, but at least half the posts should be directly related to your business. The others can be local event announcements, holiday posts, etc. If at any time you get stuck, look at your competitors. Do not copy them, but you should absolutely keep up with what they are posting about, how they roll out their specials and deals, how they make announcements, etc. Modeling your work after companies that you admire will set you up for success.

These planned posts ensure that you've got content posting on a regular basis, but don't be afraid to post on the fly too.

Examples of "on-the-fly" posts:

•If your mayor comes into your store or restaurant and you take a picture with her, absolutely post that right away! Something as simple as "Look who came in today!" and the photo will do a great job of capturing the moment.

•If you get up before dawn for an early job and catch a beautiful sunrise, take a photo and post it! Something like "Getting up at 4 a.m. is almost worth it to see beauty like this. Happy Wednesday, everyone!"

•Did someone's office get decorated for their birthday? Post a happy birthday message with the photo.

Timely posts that you catch on the fly are great additions to the posts you've already got planned. Some may just be nice quick photos for your "stories" (Instagram and Facebook), while others may seem to be fitting as an actual post. The more you get practice, the more naturally it will come to you.

A little transparency goes a long way. Make sure that you sprinkle in authentic, personal posts that help your customers get to know you. This does not mean sharing your deepest secrets (in fact, it definitely doesn't mean that). Think about what it would look like for you. Do you ski? Bicycle? Tinker with classic cars? Post a picture of you doing your hobby with text saying something like, "The best weekends are on the slopes with my family. How are you unwinding this weekend?" Not comfortable sharing too much yet? How about some behind-the-scenes images?

Did a garage full of merchandise just show up? Having a business planning meeting? Snap some photos and let your customers see what you've got going on. Don't be afraid to show a little personality.

Do you love corny jokes? Don't be afraid to be real. My friend, who owns a business, posts a good "dad joke" a couple of times a month. He gets to be his silly self, readers identify him as a goofy dad, and he gets groans or applause (i.e., engagement!) in the comments. Maybe you're obsessed with *Dancing with the Stars*—post updates about your favorite contestant or the night's performance once a week. It's just a very human way for your readers to connect with you. And the more they get to know you, the more likely they are to slow their scroll when you post about your business.

What about content for boring industries like insurance or taxes? Yes, I just called them boring so that you'll prove me wrong. A financial planner who I follow does weekly videos on specific topics in his industry that aren't boring at all! There are always new tax laws that you can share if they're applicable to your customers (stock photos will work just fine for those kinds of posts—more about that below). Maybe posting to a blog or sharing simple "fun" facts will be more in line with your industry. Whichever route you take, be sure to post regularly so the algorithm gods of social media will still give your posts attention.

If this part seemed overwhelming, please don't be discouraged. Like with most things, this gets easier with practice. Give yourself some grace and remember why you are doing this! You need to market your business, and social media is an excellent way to reach a broad audience—for free! You're halfway there on this social media assignment. You've got your account, your followers and your topics created. Next, you've got to write the post and find a picture to include.

Writing a post

If writing creative posts is your jam, right on! But if it's not, do not despair! A few key things to remember:

Keep it simple. Do not get into the details. Nobody wants to know how you're going to fix their washing machine, just that you can do it. Nobody wants to know that 1.4 oz. of color #7 mixed with 8 oz. of color #44 and a drop of #2 stirred in created that magnificent shade of gray on the house you painted.

It's all about the customer. Bottom line is this: What can you do for them? They have a problem, and they want you to fix it. You're selling their solution. Keep your post centric to your customer.

Examples:

•Is your house too hot? We'll tune up your HVAC.

•Bored this weekend? Here's a list of fun things going on in town.

•Hungry? We've got a new menu this week.

•No time for yard work? We'll mow your lawn.

•Want to keep your family safe from a fire? We'll clean your dryer vent.

Include a call to action:

•Call us for your appointment at 123-456-7890.

•For the latest menu, to see the newest merchandise, to read more about our services . . . visit our website at .

•Share this post and tell your friends about us!

Be authentic and add in some personality. Don't take yourself too seriously. People aren't just buying a product; you want them to buy *your* product. A combination of your personality, knowledge and quality product will be what they base the decision on. So don't forget the "personality" part!

Engage with your posts

The more engaged your followers are, the more reach your posts will have. If your followers like what they see, they're more likely to stop, comment, share, etc. Encourage comments by asking questions and interacting with the responses. This works with business-related and just-for-fun posts.

It's important to keep in mind that your content needs to be valuable, interesting or funny to get readers to stop their scroll. If you want them to get in the habit of engaging, your responses need to be timely. Consider a variety of these tactics and take note of how much your readers engage:

•take a poll

•ask either/or questions

•run a contest

•test their knowledge

•host an "Ask me anything about" session—let them get to know you

Example 1: Super Bowl Sunday post. Photo of all the snacks you have for the game.

Post: Got our spread ready! Be honest, are you watching for the game or the commercials?

Comment 1: The GAME! Go Niners!

Your response: YES! Go Niners! It's about time!

Comment 2: Go Dolphins!

Your response: I do like seafood! Haha kidding, my friend. May the best team win.

Comment 3: I'm here for the commercials. And the food. ALL THE FOOD.

Your response: Which was your favorite? I loved the Pepsi one!

Their response: The Ford one made me cry.

Your response: The Ford one was awesome. What was up with the chipmunk dancers? I don't even know what they were advertising.

Example 2: Hair salon post. Photos of six different haircuts.

Post: I've been busy this week! Which is your favorite? Vote below!

Comment 1: #3 because it's me!! I love this color! Thank you!

Your response: Yay! It looks beautiful on you.

Comment 2: I like #6.

Your response: Isn't her hair gorgeous? You should have seen how much we cut off! I love when my clients get bold!

Comment 3: Oh, I wish I could pull off #4.

Your response: You totally could!

Their response: Do you have any appointments coming up? I really need your help!

Encourage post shares. If your customers like your work, you hope they will tell their friends. The easiest way for them to do that is to share your posts. You can hope that they do it of their own free will, but here are some ways to make the ask.

Example 1:

Photo: work-related image

Text: Hey, happy customers! Have you told your friends about the great service you had with us? We'd love to make them a happy customer too! Would you share our post and tell your friends why our company is the best? Thanks!

Example 2:

Photo: related image

Text: We're having a sale! (Explain sale.) Friends don't let friends pay full price. Share this post and help us tell the world!

It's great when anyone shares your post, but if you've got a customer who has an influencer-size following, make a specific request for them to share your posts or to give you a shout-out. How would you know how large their social media following is? They may make it known that they are an influencer (that is, they use their social media platform to promote a product or service to potential buyers, i.e., their large group of followers). Or it may take some legwork from you to check out the accounts of your customers. This isn't a must-do, but don't pass up this opportunity if it comes to you. A customer sharing a good word about you to 10K followers is no small thing.

Photos

A word about photos—don't post bad ones. If you don't already take photos of your work, you need to start, like, yesterday. If your employees can help build a collection of photos, even better. If you have a budget, hire a professional to build a stock of photos. A professional business photographer can set up mock situations of you completing your work so you can have a collection of photos of you performing your tasks. Even if you opt for professional photos, encourage your team to take photos of their work. Did they adopt a cute stray cat they found on the job, did they plate a beautiful meal, etc. If you've got a business where the finished product sells itself, like bathroom and kitchen remodels, fitness success stories, etc., be sure you're collecting those. However you collect photos, be sure you have a variety, include staff in the pictures and only use quality ones. By quality I mean that they aren't blurry, don't show a customer's personal information, a messy home, etc.

Stock photos have their usefulness, but do not rely heavily on these. My concern with stock photos is that they can be misleading. Often it's completely obvious that they are not pictures of your actual employees or place of business. You've seen the photos of four people in business suits huddled around a stack of reports in a conference room, looking like they are discussing an important decision. Do not try to pass these off as your own employees. When it's terribly obvious that the picture isn't what you say it is, it can cause mistrust about everything else you say. In a sense, it's false advertising. It goes against all things I've said about being authentic. Your customers want to see a photo of you huddled in a booth at the local diner over cold coffee and notepads—trust me. However, it's fine to use stock photos if your messaging isn't trying to pull off that the photo is actually your work or employees. Meaning if you're posting about "summer fun activities," a photo of kids playing in the park is great. If your post is about "elderly care," a stock photo of an older couple is fine to use. Just don't post about how hard your team is working and post people who aren't your team.

Videos

If a picture is worth a thousand words, can you imagine the value of a good video? Videos historically get more views than a traditional photo on social media. It is a great way to capture the attention of your audience as they scroll. Keep your message simple and engaging, though—you want followers to actually watch it! Before filming a message, always ask, "How am I helping the customer?" rather than "How can I promote myself?" This helps ensure the viewer finds your message useful and not just marketing hype.

Are you wondering what you'll even talk about? Consider an announcement of a sale or new product or service. Show them around your new space, or give a sneak peek at some new products. People love how-to videos. A window washer who I know has made how-to videos on some of his cleaning processes. You may wonder, "Why would he give away his information like that?"

But I think it's genius. Customers who choose to use the information and wash their own windows may still choose to use him for other services or recommend him to friends. But the window washer knows that many viewers don't want to wash their own windows. Viewers are able to see how hard he works to provide quality service, and viewers may just choose to have him do the work instead.

Going "live" is a popular way to catch customers' attention in the present moment. This might be to show the excitement of a big event you've got going on or to showcase what you're working on. Some businesses do a planned live event on social media to give customers an opportunity to have a question and answer session about a service or to see the latest product launch. You've got a lot of possibilities! Don't worry about being perfect. If you're not used to being on camera, it will get easier over time. Just be yourself! If you still need ideas, view what other companies are doing for some inspiration.

When filming your video, be sure that the device you film with can shoot at a high resolution so the image is crisp. Your phone may be sufficient if it's a newer model. Be aware of the surroundings when filming so you don't expose an embarrassing situation (your messy kitchen, for example) or capture bystanders who don't want to be filmed. Unless you've got this filming thing down, no selfie videos, please.

Next step once you master your filming is to use editing software that can enhance photos and add text or your logo to your pictures and videos. You can find a lot of free, easy-to-use websites available for this, so there is a low risk to try it out.

Once you've got your video ready for viewing, you need to decide where to post it. Social channels like Facebook and Instagram have size limits, but these are great options. Your other option is YouTube. If you plan on creating a lot of videos, your posting schedule for YouTube should be included in that calendar you made. You can post on YouTube and link to it on Facebook, using your Facebook followers to drive traffic to your YouTube page. Remember to create video descriptions for your YouTube videos, much like you would on Facebook. This helps people find your video when they search for your topic. When you post videos to social media, they are mostly only viewed the day or week that you post them. If your video is just a "Hey, we've got pizza on sale today," then social media is the only place you should post that video. But if you're spending time on a how-to video or creating evergreen material, post to YouTube too. This way you can refer people back to these videos whenever you want to mention the topic again.

Storage

As you build your collection of photos and videos, store them together. There is nothing more maddening than doing all that work only to have some saved on your phone, some in email, some on your desktop, etc. Personally, I use a folder in my Google Drive. This way they are easily shareable with anyone who needs them and they are all in the same place. There are plenty of photo storage options. If you need more storage space or more security, there are paid options too. Just be sure to choose one to eliminate wasting time looking for your pictures each time you need them.

Scheduling content

At this point, you should feel very accomplished. If all goes as planned, you now have a calendar for the following month with 12 posts of photos/videos and text. If you're using Facebook and Instagram, the easiest way to schedule these in advance is through Facebook in the Meta Business Suite. Since it interfaces with Instagram, you can schedule your post to appear on both sites on the days and times you choose. Several websites offer social media planning and scheduling, but most cost money. That's not to say that they aren't useful, but if you're just getting started, I recommend choosing the simplest route to begin. As you begin to use social media, you'll notice that certain days and times of day get more engagement than others. Use this information to guide what days and times you schedule your content to post.

Wow. You just did a lot of hard work. If you hyperventilated when you realized that you must do this again next month and the one after that as well, take a deep breath.

Break down the tasks into bite-size pieces:

•Build your calendar.

•Collect your photos. (Once you build up your collection, you'll already have them to choose from. You can repeat photos so long as you don't do it too often.)

•Write your posts, which can be super simple if that works best for you. (Just be sure your posts include a call to action!)

The more you go through this process, the more habitual it will feel. And by all means, do not waste this content you're creating. You can build off of it and use it in multiple places. If you have a newsletter, your topics and posts each month should correspond. Use your material across all of your social sites, formatting however it is best. And don't forget about your website. The photos, videos and text you create can be used to enhance your website as well.

Social media posting checklist

•Create your calendar. (Goal is a minimum of 12 posts per month.)

•Capture photos/videos. (Take clear photos/quality videos.)

•Write captions. (Almost always include a call to action like "Read more on our website" with a link or call for an appointment, etc.)

•Follow your schedule. (Pay attention to your metrics to determine the best days and times to post.)

KEY TAKEAWAY: Social media is manageable if I follow the outline to plan and create content.

☐ I know what social channels I want to learn to use. This is where I need to begin the process:

Paid marketing

In this section, we'll discuss paid marketing options. Paid doesn't mean better, but it can mean a faster return or a bigger reach. All of the social media options we talked about are free, but they all have paid advertising options. Yelp is free, but there are paid advertising options with that too. I absolutely think that you need to have your social media presence and review pages solidified before moving on to more complex strategies. But there are a lot of paid tactics that may be just what your business needs to reach the goals you're after, so take the time to consider how each may relate to your business.

11

Your Business Website

You may consider your website just a cost of doing business and not a paid marketing tactic, which is great because you're right. In almost all cases, this is a nonnegotiable, necessary tool that you need. Perhaps your business is so busy that you disagree. I interviewed a landscaper who said he didn't have one, and since he was booked for 10 weeks solid, he didn't see a need. And maybe that was the case. But I'm operating under the assumption that more folks than not see a website as adding credibility to your business. Having a website tells your customer that you care enough about your business to put the effort into giving them a place to find information about you and you intend on staying in business long enough to go to the trouble. Even if business is fruitful now, a shift in the economy or your industry can change all of that. Putting the effort into this now will help you thrive when you need it.

Building a website takes time, but it will not go wasted. Once up and running, your website serves as an incredible tool to point customers to so that they can learn about your services, book appointments, read reviews and learn all about you in one place.

If you already have a website, fantastic! Use this information to ensure that it's meeting your customers needs. Even if technology isn't your strength, it's important that you pay attention to this section. I have seen so many small businesses suffer through bad experiences with web designers. Don't ignore what you don't understand.

Don't ignore what you don't understand.

This section will help you break down what you need and give you the questions to ask. Do not skip over parts because it's too technical. You honestly can't afford to ignore things just because you don't understand them.

Decisions to make before beginning:

•Who will build the website?

•Who will host the website?

•What information do you want to include?

Determining who will build and host your site

First, decide if you're going to build this website yourself or pay someone to do it. There are many tools and websites that can help you easily build a site, so doing it yourself is an option. Second, your website will need to be hosted, meaning it needs to live on a server in order to be live on the internet. I caution you not to use a website builder that makes you use their hosting service. My experience has been that these sites do not have the functionality that you might need down the road. As your business grows and you need e-commerce options, etc., some of these websites either can't support you or the cost for hosting becomes astronomical. The major downer is that if the company can't meet your needs, you're going to have to build your site from scratch to move to another web host. If you're hiring a professional to design your site, it's important to ask what platform they are using. A client of mine hired a web designer who uses one account to host every site that he builds. The client couldn't give anyone else access to the back end of his site because that would allow access to every site the web designer had built. He wasn't happy with his site, and yet he couldn't hire anyone new to edit it because of where it was hosted. Bottom line, it was a mess and a headache you can completely avoid. If you do choose to use a website builder/host all-in-one tool, be sure that it's created under an account just for you so that you have control over who has access to it.

I suggest you build your website with WordPress and then find your own hosting service. WordPress.org has thousands of themes to choose from and you can shop around for your host. WordPress might not be quite as intuitive and user-friendly as the all-in-one options, but I prefer its flexibility to grow and support your business.

Design

Before you begin designing your website, look at other websites. You can go back to the exercise you did when evaluating your competition, but you can look at other industries too. Look for sites that create a great user experience. This means that when people come to your website it's visually pleasing and the information they want is easy to find. You will want to choose colors that complement your logo and choose simple fonts that are easy to read.

When deciding on your layout, keep your customer in mind. What will they be looking for? Is it easy to find? Your phone number, appointment button or any other way for them to contact you should be easy to find on the front page. Nothing is more frustrating than having to spend time trying to figure out how to contact the company you're trying to give your business to.

Website maintenance

Be sure that you keep your website up-to-date. This means deleting coupons and specials after they expire. Customers love details when making decisions, so it might make sense for your business to include pricing. But if it fluctuates with the seasons or has a lot of variables, it is best to keep it off so it's not confusing or misleading.

Website content

If you're just starting, a word of caution—the hardest part is what sometimes seems to be the easiest: writing content. You know your business best, so you'd think this part is easy. But when it comes to organizing the information and deciding what you want to say, it's easy to feel overwhelmed. But we're going to work through that together, so just walk with me here.

Sample page types you might want listed in your navigation bar are:

- About Us
- Products
- Services
- Blog
- Contact Us
- Home Page

These will vary depending on your industry. I like to lay out the structure of a website with sticky notes.

Think of it as an organizational chart for your website. Once you get the navigation pages decided, use your sticky notes to write down everything that you want to go into that section. For example, when I first created my marketing business website, it had four links in the navigation bar: Home, About, Services and Contact. The sticky notes for my About page said: "bio, photo, list of clients." The Services page includes a list of my services and an explanation of "why market." After writing out all of my services on separate notes, I grouped them into categories that helped organize the information on that page. Remember that this is just an outline so that when it's time to write the content, you have direction on what you need. Depending on the complexity of your site, the notes allow you to move information around and reorganize it until it resembles a structure you're happy with. Your next step is writing the content (meaning words, descriptions, photos, explanations, etc.).

Your website is an extension of you. It should emulate all the values you stated in chapter 1. These things might be time-saving, professional, honest, straightforward, kind, etc. Keep that in mind as you build it. The content you include needs to be understood by someone who is not an expert in your field. It should also lead them to believe that you can help them. They should be able to tell you are an authority in your field but that you equally value the customer. Maybe this goes without saying, but check your spelling and use good grammar. Always have a second set of eyes review your content for errors and ease of understanding. Preferably choose someone who doesn't know your business as well as you do. Keep it simple and grow the details and information as the need presents itself or as time allows.

When writing the content, always consider SEO. SEO is basically the use of keywords and phrases in your content to boost your visibility when users search for relevant terms on the internet. Getting SEO right is arguably the best way to drive traffic to your website. But it's also not a golden ticket to success, so beware of anyone who promises you that they can get you to the top of search engine results. More on this in the "Hiring a Professional" chapter.

Measuring your website traffic

Knowing that your website is going to be the hub of your business, don't miss out on tracking your website analytics. You can get a plug-in for this on your website, but my preference is to use Google Analytics. The information it provides makes me giddy! I love measurable results and analytics helps with that.

Google Analytics will give you a snapshot of who your visitors are in terms of age and gender. They break down the days and times when your website traffic is highest (and lowest). You'll be able to see where your referrals are coming from, which I think is gold. This means that if you place a link on your Facebook page that gets clicked, the analytics will tell you how much traffic is coming from Facebook. If you are in online directories, you will be able to measure how much traffic you get from those other sites. If you are paying for any online advertisements, these analytics will help you measure if it's worth it. The analytics will also tell you which of your web pages are getting visited most. This can help you tell which products are most popular and what might need more attention. Do not miss out on this information. It can really help you shape where you place advertisements, what time you post on your social media and who your target audience is.

KEY TAKEAWAY: My website is a reflection of my business. Ensuring it's user-friendly with accurate information is a priority.

□ I will review my website to determine whether it needs improvement or build one if I don't have one.

12

Digital Marketing

You can use a variety of digital marketing: email, online ads and text messages.

Email

Most of us have email inboxes filled with advertisements and spam. Despite these unopened and deleted messages, email marketing is not dead. On the contrary, it's still an excellent way to reach people who you know are interested in your business subject matter. The key is who you send it to, what you say and how often you say it.

If you're curious why this category is in the paid marketing section, it's because I'd prefer to see you using a professional service like Mailchimp or Constant Contact instead of sending emails from your personal email account.

Building an email list captures an audience who liked you enough to inquire about you or do business with you. These are your people. This is especially huge if you are an independent contractor, like a personal trainer or hairstylist, trying to build clientele. If you switch shops, how will you let your customers know?

Your email list will come from two places. For starters, if you don't already, you should be collecting the email address of every customer. They should opt in to ensure you have their permission to send them marketing emails. This might be through a paper list at your register, through your appointment scheduling or through your payment system.

Then for those who are just inquiring about your business and want to learn more, you can collect their email address through a lead magnet, such as a free download or an appointment request. From this list of inquiries, I recommend a drip email campaign. A drip campaign is where a person signs up to learn more about your company or service, and then they get a series of emails ("dripping" into their inbox) to help them get to know your business, stay engaged and, hopefully, become a customer.

For example, if you own a fitness center, it could look like this:

•First email: A welcome email after receiving their email address

•Second email: All about your services sent two days later

•Third email: Introducing the team a few days after that

•Fourth email: A coupon that expires in 30 days sent a week later

Similarly, if you own a winery, the drip campaign might look like this:

•First email: A welcome email

•Second email: Who you are, the history of your winery, anything particular you are known for

•Third email: An explanation of the wine club

•Fourth email: An invitation and a coupon to use in the next 30 days (or week or whatever makes sense for you)

After the drip campaign is over, their email address would be added to your regular email list of those who receive the other emails that you send.

When you craft your email message, it should include an eye-catching photo and your logo and use consistent messaging so that your brand is easily recognized.

Do not send them spam, but do stay in touch. Some companies send out announcements for big events (sidewalk sale this weekend). Some write a monthly newsletter with an article of interest and a coupon or special. In the month of December, one client included a message of thanks to his customers and then added photos of his team's Christmas party. It gave customers a behind-the-scenes look at the employees outside of their uniforms and work environment. It projected the company as fun and warm people who care about their employees and enjoy each other's company. This client knew that he wasn't going to generate too many leads for his services close to Christmas, so this was a great way to keep in contact with customers without pressuring them with a sales pitch.

Can you think of what you would email your customers about? Do you think that regular emails would increase your sales? You may be able to think of your own personal examples of how email marketing has worked (or failed) on you.

Missed opportunity

Last Christmas I shopped at a holiday vendor fair and bought some jewelry from a very talented maker. The products were high quality, and I've gotten a lot of compliments when wearing them. Unfortunately, I didn't pay attention to her business name, and she didn't collect my information. I wish she had because if she'd sent me updates of her work, I definitely would have been a repeat customer. I likely would have followed her on her social channel and shared her posts with my friends who had complimented the jewelry. Instead, she missed out on all of this additional business.

Marketing email success

Example 1: Another jewelry store owner who I found online sends me emails about once a month when she adds new products, has a sale or wants to remind customers of shipping deadlines before the holidays. Her messaging is very authentic, and she says that her sales increase each time she sends one of these emails, likely because of the loyal customer base that she has built. As a recipient of these emails, I don't find them too frequent. They are just the right amount to remind me that her products make great gifts or that I should treat myself. They vary enough that I'm likely to open each one.

Example 2: I have shopped at a clothing boutique a few towns away, so it's not on my radar of somewhere that I think to go. But I love getting their emails once in a while because it reminds me that they are there.

Example 3: I even love the newsletter I get from a local realtor. He always includes one recipe with his market update. Since I know this about him and I love his style, I open his emails and stay on his list, even though I have no need for a realtor right now. So how does that help him? I can tell you that his name comes up in conversation when I make the recipe, and if I have a friend asking for a realtor, he may be who I suggest.

From these examples, you might get the impression that I love getting emails. I don't. I actually cannot stand opening my inbox after a day of not checking only to find spam waiting for me. I have unsubscribed from so many stores that I like because they send emails way too often. These frequent, sometimes daily, emails don't offer any special deals or buy-now incentives. They just include the same products as previous emails have shown me. Maybe they hope that if they throw their name in front of me enough I'll buy something, but unfortunately, their strategy backfires. When I unsubscribe, they lose the opportunity to ever sell to me through email again. So be wise with the quantity and quality of emails that you send out. You work hard to build your list, so you don't want to lose it.

Professional email tool

Using a professional email tool will help you format the message to look appealing and track the metrics of the number of emails that are opened and which links are clicked. This means don't forget to link to your website in your email! If the email you sent didn't have a high open rate, maybe your subject line needs to be more enticing. If your message was too long or not eye-catching, readers may have become unengaged without clicking any links. You'll also see how many readers unsubscribed. Sad face. Maybe they moved out of your area, maybe they no longer need a service like yours or maybe (gasp) you're sending them too many emails. If you see a large number of emails unopened or you're getting a lot of unsubscribes, have an honest conversation with yourself about the quality and quantity of the emails you're sending. Seek some advice from a peer or colleague to refine your strategy.

In addition, when you use a professional tool to send your emails, you can segment these emails by customer type if it makes sense for your industry. This might be by location or by the service they had performed. The purpose of this list is to home in on specific audiences rather than a large general list.

The one caveat here is if you're an independent contractor, you are going to have a smaller, more personal audience. If it really doesn't make sense for you to use a professional service at this time, using your personal email is OK. But please make sure it's not something left over from your youth like unicornqueen@hotmail.com. Have an email address that is either just your name or relates to your industry.

☐ I've considered how I will collect emails, what kind of emails I can send and when I would want to send them.

Text message

Why is this better than or different from email? It's a faster way to get to the customer. Some people don't check email every day, so if this is a limited-time offer, you want them to see it immediately. You have no way of knowing if your emails get sent to your customers' spam mail, but the text ensures they will see your message. As with email marketing, so long as you don't overuse this, text message marketing can be extremely effective. Dozens of web tools can help you set up these messages and send the texts at a relatively low cost.

Companies get customers to sign up for text message marketing by giving a coupon. For example: "Sign up for text messages and receive a 10% off coupon on your first order/service." Before offering a deal, consider how much you are essentially paying for that phone number. I get text message marketing from a big home goods store at least twice a week, which their budget allows for. Make sure yours does too.

The benefit of text message marketing is that people have "fear of missing out" and can't help but check their text when their phone dings. So if you just added a new line of jewelry to your Etsy store, text your customers to tell them! "New items just added! These are one of a kind, so once they're sold, they're gone forever. You work so hard, so you deserve to treat yourself!" Or maybe every Tuesday is half off floral bouquets, or bottles of wine, or $5 off car washes . . . Whatever your "thing" is, remind them! A quick reminder can just be "Hey, don't forget today is Taco Tuesday! $5 Tacos all day!"

Keep in mind that it's about helping to solve a customer's problem and not just promoting yourself. Customers can really come to appreciate these texts. It may help them make a decision about where they are going out to dinner tonight, remind them to send a gift for Mother's Day or remind them of a sale they may have not otherwise known about. The key for you is to be sure that your message offers a hook. "Get your gutters cleaned" is self-serving to you, but "Get your gutters cleaned before the big storm next week" helps the customer. "Eat at Freddie's tonight" doesn't help the customer, but "Pizzas are half off at Freddie's on Friday! Live music starts at 7" definitely helps the customer by offering a deal and notifying them of entertainment they may enjoy. Texts are great to fill your appointment books last minute too. I had a massage therapist who would send texts when she had a cancellation to fill that booking. It was incredibly successful. She found that even once she filled that spot, it triggered a reminder in the other recipients who would still schedule at a later time.

Keep in mind that it's about helping to solve a customer's problem and not just promoting yourself.

☐ Does it make sense to my clientele to use text message marketing? What messaging would make sense for my business?

Online ads

Ranking on search engines like Google does not equal sales. Getting a click doesn't add to your sales if the customer experience on the website isn't helpful. So search ranking is not a goal; it's a means to a goal.

My head spins when I consider the world of online advertising, so grab yourself a beverage and settle in. Online ads can be awesome. I keep seeing vacation home rentals advertised on my social channels. Clear blue water can stop my scroll anytime, and clearly, the social channel puppet masters have learned this about me because I've seen more vacation rental companies' advertisements. My social channels know me, they know my interests and they are giving me ads that are targeted appropriately.

I have no doubt that online ads can work. But I have seen businesses throw away so much money by not spending strategically. I have seen businesses "boost" social posts without any thought to the location or demographic they are trying to hit, and I've seen online ads that don't include a call to action or even a clear description of what they're selling. I mean, that's great if you are so flush that you can spend your money like you are playing Monopoly, but most small businesses can't. I find it incredibly unnerving to spend money on advertising without any metrics to measure your success.

So how do you avoid this?

Because we learn from repetition, I'll say it again—consider your demographic. For example, if your potential clients are under 25, you are going to do more TikTok than LinkedIn. Google and Facebook will let you narrow down interests, age, city and more, so be sure your ads are showing to the right people. Take the time to set these metrics. Otherwise, you may end up accidentally wasting precious ad dollars advertising your catering service three states away. Unless you travel for work, that's not going to help you.

A great way to help you decide where to spend your advertising dollars is by checking your analytics on your website and social channels. Who are they and where are they coming from? Are you looking to grab more of those customers or trying to reach new ones?

When you create your ad, be sure you set your demographic, use a quality image that shows off your company and make sure your ad copy clearly states what you're offering with a call to action. Remember, they have a problem, and you need to tell them how you're going to solve it. Make sure the link the ad sends them to is not your home page but rather the specific web page that fits the topic of the ad. You pulled the customer in, so don't make them search for the information.

Start small with a budget, timeline and goal to help you measure your results. Keep an eye on the progress of your ad so you can change it if necessary.

KEY TAKEAWAY: Digital marketing is a valuable way to stay in touch with my customers.

☐ If online ads make sense for my business, what do I want to promote?

13

Paid Advertising and Event Opportunities

We touched on some free options in this category of traditional advertising, but there are even more that can be paid for. Perhaps you tried the avenue of free print, radio and TV but didn't find any opportunities. Well, believe me, if there isn't a free option, you can bet there are plenty of paid.

Print, radio and television

In the previous section, we talked about finding some opportunities for free publicity in these areas, but sometimes the best tactic is to just take out a good old advertisement. This could be in a newspaper, magazine, event program or mail flyer. Some communities have welcome packets they send to new home buyers. You can pay to include your advert in their welcome packet so the new homeowners come to your neighborhood restaurant, buy their life insurance from you, visit your nail salon, etc.

Other print options are billboards and transportation. Billboards are a *big* way to reach customers but also are incredibly costly and don't target a specific demographic. Other print options include bus station advertising and advertising on public transit. Grocery carts too. Don't forget to include a coupon code for tracking.

Radio advertisements can be very effective if you're looking to hit your local area. Thinking of the demographic you want to reach, choose a station that reaches this crowd. This could be an FM music station or a local AM radio show. Most stations will create the commercial for you, so it takes a lot of pressure off you. Be sure to ask if anyone else in your industry is running a commercial at the same time to avoid that direct competition. Include a limited-time special to encourage customers to call/visit/book now.

Television advertisements can be very costly because you have to factor in the cost to produce them as well as air them. A similar and simpler solution might be movie theater advertising. Instead of having to produce a commercial, they often offer still ads to show on the screen before movies. These are still a costly investment, though. So not a no, just maybe a not yet.

☐ What specific method would work best for my business?

Events

Booths that showcase your business might make sense for your industry. It can be a great way for potential customers to meet you or your staff, ask questions and get to know you. Gaining new customers can be done by offering discounts for purchases/bookings made on-site or by passing out coupons valid for a short time to encourage the customer to make the decision to use your business soon. This is how I hired my pest company. I had heard about them, and I loved that they offered a more natural bug spray solution, but I had questions, and I thought they would be too expensive. We already had a pest service, and with being busy with work, being a mom, etc., hiring a new company was not my priority. If they hadn't been at this home show, I'm not sure if I ever would have hired them. My husband and I went to the home show to learn about remodeling our kitchen, but dozens of different industries were represented. The two men working the pest company booth were very approachable with great personalities. They answered my questions like I was talking to a friend, not a salesman. When we got to the cost part, I told them they were a lot more than my current service (albeit they had a better product). They were able to offer me an "event only" special if we signed up on the spot. The commitment was month to month, so we really had nothing to lose. Their approach, knowledge and cost flexibility got them the sale (and probably many more after me). That's what you're going for.

Events are an excellent complement to the marketing you are already doing. If you're focusing your advertising on a certain demographic, like advertising in a 55+ community magazine, setting up a booth at their next event can clinch the business. Maybe they've seen your ad and perhaps their neighbor has already used your business, but meeting you in person can be exactly what the customer needs to make their decision. If your focus is a certain city or town, look for event opportunities to complement the marketing you already do in that area. Nothing beats the authenticity of meeting you in person.

Types of events:

•community events, especially around holidays

•retirement community vendor fairs

•industry conferences

•chamber of commerce events

•job fairs

•fairs and festivals

□ What kind of events would be appropriate for my business?

Host an event

If you can't find an event to be a part of, host an event yourself! A local realtor hosts happy hour events every quarter, and they are so successful. I drove by their parking lot during an Octoberfest celebration and thought, "Wow, I wish I was invited!" They capitalize on past customers and invite contacts they've made at open houses. It's a fun social occasion that builds customer loyalty with new and past clients. I've also seen salons have anniversary celebrations where they invite the entire community, offering guests a chance to learn more about services and a chance to win products.

Is there a topic your customers would like to hear about at a free seminar? You can make it enticing by offering food, discounts, etc. This might be an opportunity to partner with another local business. Think of related partnerships like a veterinarian/dog trainer/pet store or even just having a new food truck to help get their name out as well. Not only will these events help you build your email contact list, but they also give you one-on-one face time with potential customers, which is priceless.

□ Could I host an event that potential and past customers would like to attend? Are there other companies I can partner with to help make my event a success?

Sponsorships

Community events may have sponsorship opportunities, and dozens of other types of events look for business sponsors. These events may offer you signage posted, social media attention, your logo on their website or your name in their program or on a T-shirt. These events vary in subject matter and price range. Look for events whose crowds fit your customer demographic and budget. You may find that the nonprofit organizations you support are in need of event sponsors, and this can be an excellent opportunity to both support an organization you care about and advertise your business.

When deciding how to sponsor an event, choose any opportunity that will display your logo on a banner. Long-term sponsorships like your local baseball league or high school sports team will have visitors staring at your business name at every game for weeks at a time. These repeat impressions are valuable. If it's at a one-day event, the more your name is mentioned or your logo is seen, like posted prominently or printed on every napkin, the more you will be remembered.

Potential events to sponsor:

•crab feeds

•5K runs

•high school sports

•local semiprofessional sports

•community fairs and festivals

☐ What kinds of events would I like to sponsor?

Chamber of commerce and other associations

Your local chamber of commerce can be a great asset. But it only helps you if you join! Chambers of commerce offer businesses access to resources, discounts and relationships with like-minded individuals. A quality chamber has regular meetings for members to network and share about their services. These meetings offer a group of peers who can help support you not only with business referrals but also as other business owners who may be going through the same things that you are. These people will get you; they'll understand the hard work you do. Here you may find a mentor or become one for somebody else. If talking to strangers or presenting to groups isn't your strength, bring an employee for support. And bring those business cards and flyers!

Your local chamber of commerce can be a great asset.

You can join dozens of other groups to help you network. Most people don't have time to join all of them, but consider what matters to you and what you find most helpful. Is there an association for your trade? Or perhaps a local business owner group that you identify with, like "Christian Business Owners" or "Women in Business"? These groups won't necessarily help with your marketing directly, but they can be a helpful resource to learn from others' experiences, like their marketing and outreach successes.

☐ Is there a local chamber of commerce or association that I should join?

KEY TAKEAWAY: Traditional forms of advertising are great ways to reach a large audience.

14

Printed Marketing Material

Whether you're a website designer, insurance salesman or life coach, chances are you have a business card. This might just be the start of the marketing materials that you have printed to promote your business. Be sure that all of your printed material and advertisements use a consistent logo, colors and messaging (i.e. integrated marketing). This is your brand identity. It's confusing to customers if your business card has pink flowers but the logo on your car is black and yellow. The consistency makes you recognizable and, therefore, makes an impression. A study from Loyola University suggests that color increases brand recognition by 80 percent.

Remembering those eight impressions you're trying to make, think of where else you can put your logo.

Business cards and flyers

Business cards are an easy tool to pass along your contact information. They are inexpensive and relatively easy to design. Many different printing companies have online tools for you to design the card yourself.

Flyers and brochures make excellent, inexpensive marketing tools for most businesses. Remember to keep the color and style in line with your branding. Be sure to include what your business does and methods to contact you. If you're a personal chef, be sure to include any other services you offer, like catering or meal planning. If you're a day spa, include a summary of your services and packages. Pricing and details can be included, or you can direct them to your website for that information. If you're having a booth at an event, you want to have a flyer and/or brochure to give customers something to take home to remember you.

A flyer or postcard is a great tool to sell additional products when you are at a customer's home. A window washer might have a "rack card" (4x8 postcard) that on one side has general business information and on the backside lists the specific services they offer in addition to window cleaning, like power washing or gutter cleaning. Whichever service the technicians are performing, they are sure to tell the customer about their other services and leave them the card. It serves as a great reminder after they leave for the customer to use them again. While the same information could be included on a business card, the rack card can fit more information, is in larger print and is less likely to get misplaced like a small business card might.

☐ How can I utilize flyers and brochures in my business?

Car wraps

Do your company cars have your logo on them? If your budget allows, consider this, as cars that are wrapped in a design and logo are eye-catching. Whether it's just your company name and logo or it's a full colorful wrap, be sure that your business name and contact information are clear, professional and large enough to read. This one-time cost provides countless impressions, as the cars are driven each day and parked in front of customers' homes. Neighbors may see your vehicle and choose to call your business just based on the fact that their neighbor trusted you. If your car is blank, they'll never know who you were.

☐ Does this apply to my business?

Yard signs

I love yard signs for home services. For example: These windows were cleaned by [insert company name]; We're CHILLIN' because our AC was tuned up by [insert company name]; This house was painted by [insert company name]. So often people want recommendations for services, but they don't know who to ask. When it comes to their home, who better than their neighbors? Often it gives them the idea to use a service that they haven't even thought of. Imagine a sign in a yard that says: My solar panels are catching more rays because I had them cleaned by [insert company name]. A neighbor thinks, "Wait, they had their solar panels cleaned? We're supposed to have them cleaned? Shoot, OK, I better have it done too." Think of how these signs can add to your impressions. If that cleaning company had employees canvass the same neighborhood with flyers after the service, the other homeowners would not only see the sign in the neighbor's yard but they'd also be able to connect the name with the friendly employee who stopped by their home.

☐ Is this a tool I can utilize?

Swag

If you're setting up a booth of any kind, you probably want some swag to give away. It attracts visitors to your table and can make great conversation starters. Simple giveaways like a pen or a notepad will keep your logo front and center each time someone uses it. To this point, I just came across a pen for a private investigator in my junk drawer. I thought, "Where on earth did I pick that up?" It's a great pen, though! Not your cheap 15¢ variety but the kind with a stylus on the end and a rubber grip. So I googled the business name. I didn't recognize the woman, and I still don't know where the pen came from. But it made an impression. And should I ever need a private investigator, her hope is that memory is triggered.

I don't think you can go wrong with swag; just consider your audience. If it's a summer day, fans with your company logo are a big hit. Reusable bags are popular, and I will take a quality "chip clip" from any booth. I can't get enough of those! If you can find things that make sense for your industry, that's helpful too. Washer repair companies put a magnet on the washers they service to remind you to call them the next time an appliance breaks down. Beauty salon? Put your contact info on a nail file. Maybe next time they file their nails, they'll realize they really need a professional manicure, and they'll come see you. Keeping your budget in mind, remember that they are just tools to help make impressions, not likely the thing that will seal the deal.

KEY TAKEAWAY: Printed materials are great assets. It's important to keep cohesive branding throughout all of the material we create.

□ Which items would best serve my business?

15

Hiring a Professional

If some of this is beyond your scope of time or knowledge, you should absolutely hire help. Paying to have your website built is better than not having one! But if you're going to do this, you need to understand what you're paying for.

Like having your own baby, you know your business best. While it's important to consult experts, don't ever let someone talk you into something that feels wrong to you.

I have heard heartbreaking stories of business owners who got taken advantage of because they didn't do their research. It's not your fault for trusting a professional. You don't know what you don't know. But it is your responsibility to learn enough before hiring a marketing firm or website designer.

I knew a small business owner who had a company offer to make his SEO so good that he'd be in the top Google searches in his industry for just $45,000, and it would only take 9–18 months to see results. The sales pitch was so convincing that he really contemplated spending the money. It sounded so appealing, but friends, his marketing budget before this was next to nothing. And he didn't understand that many of the things this offer included were things he could easily do himself. Not to mention, as discussed earlier, being at the top of the search does not guarantee you increased sales. This isn't to say that an "SEO expert" can't help you, but it's important to know exactly what you're getting for the price you're paying.

Unfortunately, a lot of people will oversell and overcharge because they hope you don't know better. I talked to an ice cream shop owner who was paying $2,000 a month to a mailer service to send out his coupons. This shouldn't cost that much! Not to mention what it cost him to sell his product at a lower cost when the customers used the coupon. Another scam that really makes my blood boil is illegitimate "best of" contests. I have seen scams where an organization contacts a business to say, "You won best coffee shop/museum/housekeeping service, etc. in the area! Just pay us $X amount of money, and you can get a plaque to hang in your business. Upgrade to the premium package, and we'll tell our whole social media following that you won!" Excuse me, what? Could you imagine if a school went to a teacher and said, "You won teacher of the year. Pay us money and we'll put it on a plaque, and if you want us to tell everyone on social media, pay us double?' What? No. Do not pay someone to tell you how great you are. You're going to prove that all on your own.

This book was written to help put those scammers out of business. I want you to have the confidence that you can do this and that it's worth your efforts. Of course, not everyone is out to swindle you; I just want you to be aware. If you decide to pay for web or marketing services, shop around, ask for referrals and ask them questions. Ask lots of questions. Get a second opinion. You really can't afford to do it any other way.

Questions to ask your professional:

•What is your experience with businesses similar to mine? (Hopefully they have some.)

•What kind of research will you do on my business? (They should take the time to get to know you and your business to best reflect your business.)

•Do you work in-house or outsource your projects? (In-house is definitely preferred.)

•Can you design my [brochure, website, etc.] within my budget? (Be sure they are up front about pricing.)

•How long will this take? (Make sure the timeline fits your needs.)

•How many edits/revisions are included? (Be sure to understand if there are fees associated with changes.)

•For websites: Do I own the site and contents? (It is important that you do.)

•For websites: What kind of training/support do you provide? (If you will be managing your website after it's designed, you may need this.)

KEY TAKEAWAY: If I need to hire a marketing professional, it's important to research the company and appropriate amount the service will cost.

☐ I will do my research and ask for referrals before I agree to hire a marketing professional.

Part 3

Your Marketing Strategy

You've almost completed every component of your marketing plan. You've identified your business, your audience, your competition, your goals and your budget, and you've learned multiple strategies to market your business. This final part is deciding which strategies you're going to apply.

After digesting dozens of free and paid marketing options, I hope you're brimming with ideas to market your business. Revisit your notes to determine which strategies appeal to you. Are you ready to dive into social media? Or maybe you're excited to start having a booth at community events?

Next, take inventory of what really makes sense for your industry. What kinds of opportunities exist that are relevant to your business? This is a time to think critically about what your business needs and what you can realistically afford.

Before you prioritize your marketing strategies, review your answers in part 1 so your marketing decisions are in line with your business priorities.

16

Implementing Marketing Strategies

Each business is going to be a little different, but it's a good bet to get set up with your free social accounts and a Google Business Profile. If you already have these, now is a great time to revisit them for accuracy and consistency. Get your free business services dialed in while contemplating other marketing you want to explore.

Time commitment

You committed to reading this book, so I can assume you're committed to marketing your business. Remember that this means that you need to make room in your schedule for your marketing to be successful. A good rule of thumb for your social media accounts is to spend about four–five hours planning out a month of posts and getting them scheduled.

Then you need to plan time for all that goes into marketing. For example, working a booth at an event requires time for booth prep (ordering swag, brochures, supplies, etc.) and the time you will spend working the booth. I don't point these things out to scare you but to prepare you. You are very capable of every task listed in this book. Implemented correctly, your business will be better for all of the time you spend on marketing.

□ I have set aside time in my schedule to make marketing a priority.

Measuring success

The marketing for your business is already better because you committed to educate yourself and evaluate your business needs. When paying for marketing, it's helpful to have measurable results. So as you try each strategy, be sure to include a method for measuring your results when possible. Are coupon codes being redeemed, is your website getting more traffic or, most importantly of all, are you achieving your overall goals?

One way to measure results is to offer a coupon code attached to your advertisement. For example: Mention you heard about us on the *Money Talk Show* and save 10%! Or include a coupon code on a print advertisement unique to the advertisement so you can keep track of how many customers you got from that method of advertising. If you hand out flyers at events, be sure the coupon attached is unique to the event so you know where the business came from. If you can't offer a coupon, your tracking could be something like: Tell us you saw us in the paper and be entered into a drawing. Or: We'll give our nonprofit partner $5 for every customer they refer to us. The discount that you offer on a coupon does affect your bottom line, so that should be factored into your marketing budget.

Unfortunately, measurable results are not a surefire plan to know what method works best. If it takes eight impressions for a consumer to recognize you, that could mean that even if they respond to a Facebook ad, that might not be what really attracted them to you. When I began marketing for the theater, they were relatively small. My goal was to make them a household name and to stop being asked if we were "that theater downtown" (which was our competition). We grew exponentially in my time there, but can we really say why? We had booths at a lot of local events. We took advantage of free TV appearances. We paid for advertising in a local magazine. We had a busy social media presence. The website was full of information. But it's hard to say if *one* thing was really our golden ticket to success. So keep in mind that while measurable is great, overall growth is the goal.

Your marketing success will depend largely on the consistent monitoring of your results, your patience and your flexibility.

Your marketing success will depend largely on the consistent monitoring of your results, your patience and your flexibility.

The strategy you set your heart on may not work, and that's OK. Success is measured by how you pivot and begin again, each time a little wiser than before. Keeping to your core values and remembering your *why* will lead you to the success you desire.

☐ I will measure my results and monitor overall growth of my business.

Next steps

Whether you're overwhelmed or excited to get started, my advice is to start small. That's great if you want to do it all, but pick one strategy to begin to focus on. If you're spending money in multiple places, monitoring the results gets time-consuming. If you start small, it's easier to expand strategically.

Get out a blank piece of paper or download the next steps worksheet from thejenadvantage.com. With your business evaluation and all of the other exercises you've completed, consider the first strategy you want to explore and how it will support your overall goals. Creating a SMART goal, list specific next steps for the next 30 days.

Perhaps your first strategy is to start using your social media regularly. A SMART goal might be something like this: I want to start using social media by spending one hour per week to create 12 posts each month so I can let more consumers know about my business. Your task list may include things like this:

•Update social media accounts with a consistent profile photo and business information.

•Gather all of your business photos in one file.

•Brainstorm posting ideas.

•Develop a posting calendar to fill in each month.

•Monitor customer engagement on social media to determine the best time of day to post.

Revisit the guidance given in each strategy section if you need help remembering what needs to be done. When your task list is complete, continue creating SMART goals related to your marketing strategies for the next 90 days and one year. Your strategies may change as you evaluate your tactics over time, but regardless, your strategies should all relate to your overall goals from your business evaluation.

If you've completed all of the exercises in this book, you are ready to implement your marketing plan. You've worked hard to get to this point, and you should be proud. Keep this book and all of your notes accessible to revisit on occasion. If your business begins to expand or launches a new product or the industry begins to change, revisit your plan and make adjustments if needed. It may be time to add a new strategy. Continue to measure your results, and remember, marketing is a process, not an event. You've got this!

Cheers to your successful marketing!

☐ I have created my first marketing strategy task list and I am ready to begin!

Sources

Chapter 5

Evans, Michael. "6 Steps to Developing a Small Business Marketing Budget." *Forbes*, May 2, 2017. https://www.forbes.com/sites/allbusiness/2017/05/02/6-steps-to-developing-a-small-business-marketing-budget/?sh=67db02b9355c.

Chapter 7

97% of consumers consult reviews: "The Growing Power of Reviews: How Consumer Dependence on Ratings and Reviews Continues to Evolve." Power Reviews. 2018. https://www.powerreviews.com/wp-content/uploads/2018/03/The-Growing-Power-of-Reviews.pdf.

Chapter 10

3 billion Facebook users, 2 million active daily. 24% of Facebook's audience is 18–24: Beveridge, Claire. "19 Facebook Demographics to Inform Your Strategy in 2022." Hootsuite. March 24, 2022. https://blog.hootsuite.com/facebook-demographics/.

More than two-thirds of users are under 35: "Distribution of Instagram Users Worldwide as of April 2022, by

Age Group." Statista. https://www.statista.com/statistics/325587/instagram-global-age-group/.

Users spend an average of 53 minutes on the site each day: Molla, Rani and Wagner, Kurt. "People Spend Almost as Much Time on Instagram as They Do on Facebook." Vox. June 25, 2018. https://www.vox.com/2018/6/25/17501224/instagram-facebook-snapchat-time-spent-growth-data.

With over 2 billion users: Market.us. "YouTube Statistics and Facts." Market.us. Updated November 24, 2021. https://market.us/statistics/online-video-and-streaming-sites/youtube/.

Viewers retain when they watch a video compared to 10% when reading it in text: "50 Must-Know Stats about Video Marketing 2016." Insivia. Accessed June 10, 2022. https://www.insivia.com/50-must-know-stats-about-video-marketing-2016/.

72% of customers would rather learn about a product or service by way of video than alternatives like text or infographics: Hayes, Adam. "What Video Marketers Should Know in 2022, According to Wyzowl Research." HubSpot. Updated May 6, 2022. https://blog.hubspot.com/marketing/state-of-video-marketing-new-data.

Videos generate: Sanghavi, Aayushi. "40 Video Marketing Statistics to Boost Your Video Strategy." G2. January 31, 2022. https://www.g2.com/articles/video-marketing-statistics.

With just over 2 million daily active users: "Q4 2021 Letter to Shareholders." Twitter. February 10, 2022 https://s22.q4cdn.com/826641620/files/doc_financials/2021/q4/Final-Q4'21-Shareholder-letter.pdf.

99% of Twitter users also use at least one other social media network: "Digital 2020: October Update." Hootsuite. October 2020. https://www.hootsuite.com/resources/digital2020-q4-update.

Chapter 14

Color increases brand recognition by 80 percent: Santo, Alexander. “How to Increase Brand Awareness with Impressions Marketing.” *Brafton* (blog). December 11, 2019. https://www.brafton.com/blog/strategy/how-to-increase-brand-awareness-with-impressions-marketing/.

Acknowledgments

When I began my own marketing agency I quickly found that my biggest struggle was that I would be limited to how many people I could help. Hence my two passions—writing and helping small businesses—came together to create this book. It could not have been done without the support from my coach, Kerk Murray. Kerk, your patience, faith and encouragement was instrumental to me finishing this book. Thank you to my editor Katie Chambers from Beacon Point LLC and my proofreader Laura Majors. Both were so helpful and excellent in their craft.

To my friend Alisa Russell, not only for our timeless friendship but for your input and advice along the way.

I am grateful for my clients; for the trust they put in me and the referrals they send my way. I may be your expert in marketing, but I have learned so much from each of you.

My admiration for entrepreneurs not only comes from watching my clients but also from every passionate small business owner I meet, specifically through the Roseville Chamber of Commerce. The Chamber provides the finest support and encouraging environment to be a small business owner.

Thank you to my kids for constantly speaking words of encouragement over me. How could I tell you to follow your dreams if I didn't follow my own? You inspire me.

And my husband Joe, thank you for the support you continually offer me. Not everyone has a spouse that supports and affirms dreams like you do and I know just how blessed I am to have you.

About the Author

Jen Esparza has spent her career in the creative industry and has provided marketing for a variety of campaigns running the gamut from government programs to children's theater. As the owner of an agency that focuses on marketing for small businesses and nonprofits, she appreciates the hardworking entrepreneur and has an unwavering passion to help them succeed. Trusted by her clients and inspired by the celebration of their successes, she has written this book to help assist more small business owners achieve their goals through successful marketing.

Jen lives in Northern California with her husband and two children.

LET'S CONNECT!

I really hope this book has helped you feel more confident about marketing your small business.

Remember that part about the importance of reviews? I would really appreciate you writing one about the book! I love hearing what you have to say and appreciate your feedback. Plus it might help a fellow small business owner decide to read the book and help them like it has helped you! Review on your favorite book-buying website like Amazon.

SOCIAL MEDIA:
FACEBOOK AND INSTAGRAM

@thejenadvantage

Printed in Great Britain
by Amazon